WHY ME?

A Look at One Life – Mine

Anthony Salter

Group Captain RAF Retired

MAPLE
PUBLISHERS

WHY ME?

Author: Anthony Salter

Copyright © Anthony Salter (2025)

The right of Anthony Salter to be identified as author of this work has been asserted by the author in accordance with section 77 and 78 of the Copyright, Designs and Patents Act 1988.

First Published in 2025

ISBN 978-1-83538-594-4 (Paperback)
978-1-83538-636-1 (E-Book)

Book cover design and layout by:
White Magic Studios
www.whitemagicstudios.co.uk

Published by:
Maple Publishers
Fairbourne Drive, Atterbury,
Milton Keynes,
MK10 9RG, UK
www.maplepublishers.com

A CIP catalogue record for this title is available from the British Library.

All rights reserved. No part of this book may be reproduced or translated by any form or by any means, electronic or mechanical, including photocopying, recording or by any information storage and retrieval system without written permission from the author.

This book is a memoir. It reflects the author's recollections of experiences over time. Some names and characteristics have been changed, some events have been compressed, and some dialogues have been recreated, and the Publisher hereby disclaims any responsibility for them.

WHY?

I have no doubt that all of us at some time have asked ourselves the question, "Why?" Things happen to us in life which are hard to explain, some are good (hopefully most) some are bad, some are the result of our own actions, some seem just random and really nothing to do with us at all. There also good people to whom bad things happen, and bad people who seem to only have good things happen to them, and after a while we are left with the conclusion that life isn't fair. And it isn't, but that is not the point. The point is what do we do with them, these things that happen, how we react to them and how we act thereafter. My life has been no different to anyone else's in that respect, except that I think that I may have been a slower learner. So what I have tried to do here is look objectively at my life, which has been long and very full, and weigh the good and the bad together. This is by no means an ego trip but the result of finally giving in to the persuasion of friends, who for many years now, have wanted me to try and record the factual verbal stories they have heard me tell. I do it with my tongue in my cheek, not really feeling that my life is any more commendable or interesting than anyone else's, which is true although it may have been a little different and out of the ordinary. I love to listen to the life stories of others, even those who feel that because they have lived in one place and put down roots, they have done nothing of real value. Yet when you listen to them you realise that although they may not have travelled the world or done spectacular things, they have built a structure called 'family and friends' which is large and cohesive and have thus put so much into the community around them, which is commendable and is something I have never been in one place long enough to do. All I hope is that there may be something of interest here for you and you will not be bored!

In the beginning

It was a Friday and I have it on good authority that it was raining as I arrived at about 8 am that morning. No wonder I have never been that fond of rain and getting wet, but there may not be any connection and it may have been other fluids that established the feeling. However, in later life it did not stop me becoming very at home in the water as a swimmer and diver. So there

I was on the 15th June in 1934 a small noisy lump of humanity no doubt wondering what on earth I was doing there, something I have been trying to work out ever since. Hence the question, "Why Me?"

It is surprising how much you can remember from your days as a small child: unconnected and insignificant events they may have seemed at the time, but no doubt they had an influence on how I was to view later life. The window cleaner who played hide and seek with me, the steam traction engine driving the threshing machine connected by a huge belt in the field across the main A25 road from our house in Sevenoaks in Kent; me as a five year old wading into a group of boys who were bullying my older brother, and them being completely stunned by this whirling dervish with arms and fists everywhere; being knocked over by a car just yards from our house and looking at my mangled right leg with my foot sticking out sideways instead of pointing forwards, and the driver saying that she just did not see me which seemed very strange to me at the time, since I fell on the grass verge at the side of the road with my leg trapped under her left front wheel; the dark gloom that descended on the garden where we were having tea as war with Germany was announced on the radio in 1939; being in hospital in 1940 having my tonsils out and from my bed watching a Me 109 in a tight left turn round the bluff the hospital stood on; watching the glow from the north as London burned from the blitz; even as a child I was aware of the legacy of WW1 by the number of disabled ex-servicemen selling items or begging on the streets, no Welfare State in those days. Even though only a small child I was not immune from the unpleasantness and cruelty of war, and just walking to school in Sevenoaks when only 6 or 7 years old, I passed a crashed German bomber from the raid the night before, which was burnt out and from the pungent and acrid smell it was obvious to me that the crew, or at least their bodies, were still in it. I was to meet that smell again in India thirty plus years later, but on a much larger scale. On another occasion I passed a line of army trucks beside which was lying a soldier who had obviously been crushed between the tailboards of two trucks that had reversed into each other. He, poor chap, was a mess and with hindsight it is hard to see how, even with modern medicine, his body could have been reassembled for all his innards were just hanging out.

WHY ME?

My Father and neighbours had built a substantial shelter in our back garden which would probably have survived all but a direct hit. It would accommodate about twelve people and during 1941 we spent more nights in it than in our own beds!

Moving to Maidstone in 1942 and having to make new friends was a challenge. Maidstone was and is the County Town of Kent and had a very good Grammar School. I was enrolled in the preparatory class in September 1942 and my older brother joined too but a year ahead of me. We lived to the North of the Town and the school was to the South and this involved cycling two and a half miles each way. This gave me the opportunity to stop and watch the aerial dogfights going on in the skies above me as the RAF took on the Nazi hordes, and I was oblivious to the shrapnel falling all around me. Maidstone was surrounded by fighter airfields, West Malling, Detling, Headcorn, Biggin Hill etc, and so there was always some activity both day and night. On one occasion a friend and I were witnesses to a Spitfire making a forced landing just a few hundred yards from us. We had seen it coming down and rushed to intercept it. The prop was not turning so either the engine had malfunctioned or it had run out of fuel, most likely the latter. Unfortunately, it clipped a hedge just before hitting the ground and flipped over onto its back thus trapping the pilot who could not open the canopy. Thank God there was no fire which reinforced my idea of running out of fuel and the pilot was probably trying to make it to West Malling which was only a short distance away. My friend, Mcleod sadly died a short time after this with a perforated appendix which developed into peritonitis.

My bicycle was very important to me and took me all over the local area even though it was a heavy old Raleigh but we had freedom to explore our local area out to a radius of about fifteen miles. Rushing to crash sites before they were closed and getting used to the distinctive smell of aircraft was exciting, although some smells were not so pleasant when dead bodies were a result of the crash as I had already realised. In 1944 I watched the first Meteor jet fighters formatting on and toppling the gyros of doodlebugs (V1s), little realising at that time that eleven years later I would be flying the Meteor 8, a later version of the aircraft I was watching. I joined the School CCF (Combined Cadet

Force) RAF section and in 1949 had my first hands-on flight in a Tiger Moth operated by an Air Experience Flight at Rochester airport. Together with gliding and operating the winches and tow trucks at the Detling gliding school, this gave me an ambition to become a pilot which conflicted with my Headmaster's wish that I go to university and study Law. We also frequented the church youth clubs which is where the young people gathered, and this, plus church attendance, gave us a basic understanding of religion. The town also had a very good girl's Grammar School and a Technical School and there was quite a lot of mixing between the three, and the girls always beat us at hockey sometimes using tactics and sticks in an unauthorised way , and we found that it is hard to run with a hockey stick round your ankle, but it was all good fun.

In 1949 my brother Michael got his motorbike license and bought a Francis Barnett. This gave us added mobility and shortened journey times so that we were able to get jobs in the summer holidays on a local fruit and veg farm. It was hard work in the fields hoeing and harvesting root vegetables, cabbage and beetroot. Some of the beetroot would grow abnormally large, about twelve inches in diameter, and not being suitable for the greengrocery trade, we were allowed to take them home where they were cut up, boiled and eaten. The only down side was that our packed lunches would be cheese and beetroot sandwiches for days afterwards. The fruits were apples and we were tasked each day last thing in the afternoon before quitting, to help load the ten ton truck with bushel boxes of apples due to leave in the early hours of the next morning bound for Covent Garden market. We learnt the trick of the trade lifting these boxes eight high before strapping them securely. What Health and Safety would think of all this now I hate to think but we became quite competent at what we were given to do. Fortunately we were both quite big and strong thanks to our sporting activities. In the shorter holidays we worked in a local fruit canning factory either sorting the damaged cans before they reached the labelling machine, or packing boxes at the other end of the conveyer. All good experience, useful pocket money, and a sense of satisfaction.

My parents were not religious, but my mother encouraged my brother and me to attend church, get confirmed, go to Sunday school, and join Crusaders, which was a sort of non-denominational bible school. It also ran summer camps so we were able to see more of the country than most kids, and we did learn some of the principles for good living, although like most kids I had a tendency to forget them at crucial moments, like thumping a bully when I couldn't stand anymore. It stopped the bullying though! I found some relief when feeling troubled, by cycling out to Boxley, leaving my bike by the church, and walking up the slopes of the North Downs and lying in the long grass, watching the ever-changing clouds, and listening to the breeze making music in the long grass. Perhaps one varying note with harmonics but it was very peaceful. Obviously weather dependent! By 1946 I had started playing the oboe which I loved, and played in the school orchestra (the oboe was on loan from the school) and various chamber music groups. I was competent and fairly good, but not gifted. Even so my parents got me a professional teacher and I improved a great deal. I did consider making it a vocation but was advised against it since it was a hard road to the top, and very few make it and reap the financial rewards. In the war years and immediately after I did not do well at school, being unable to focus and work. It was a combination of lacklustre teaching and my wandering mind! Despite this my parents stood up for me and were pleased to see the belated transformation, since all this changed early in 1947 when we got a new form master and German teacher, German being one of my subjects. Mr Gilpin had been a Colonel in the Army, but it wasn't what he said or did so much as what he was – an example! He had a profound influence on me probably without knowing it, and I went from bottom five to top five in one term. I just thank God for that man.

In my later teens I retired the old Raleigh and built myself, what was at that time, a state of the art much lighter weight racing bike. I began to cover much longer distances and eighty miles in an afternoon was quite common, and I got to know Kent very well. Cycling from Maidstone to Lincolnshire in a day was a common challenge and then on to Chesterfield to visit my maternal grandparents, and then on again to Sheffield to stay with my aunt Olive, for with much less traffic in those days and the blessings of transport cafes, life was relatively safe and simple. I entered the occasional race but never really got hooked, much preferring exploring on my own. In fact, doing a fifty-mile road race in less than two hours was an achievement but hurtling down steep Sussex hills, such as round Crowborough, in the midst of a pack of cycles doing speeds approaching fifty miles per hour, did not really appeal. The clash of one pedal with someone else's spokes would spell disaster. In those days no one wore a helmet or protective clothing for they were not available! By this time, I was also a very proficient swimmer much helped by the school having an outdoor, unheated, pool. I have found that my times in unheated pools are always much faster than in heated pools. Fortunately my racing distances were up to two hundred yards, so hyperthermia did not have time to kick in!

RAF College Cranwell

Early in 1952 I took the Civil Service Qualifying exam, which was the first step in getting selected for the RAF College at Cranwell for which I had applied earlier. That spring and summer were taken up with various selection tests to make sure that I had the right qualities and aptitude, and much to my delight I came through without a hitch. And so on a day in early September 1952 I caught the train to Grantham and was coached to Cranwell where I joined C Squadron No 64 Entry. The initial basic training was tough and designed to make men out of boys. Our initial accommodation was the 'lines' a line of huts erected during WW1 which was our home of the first two terms. Basically, we were all Aircraftsmen 2nd Class (AC2), and you cannot get any lower! Some of the equipment that was issued was very much WW2 including fur lined boots, leather gauntlets, and leather flying helmets, now worth a fortune at auction. It was a tough regime, very early mornings, late nights, and everything had to be spotless and meticulously laid out as per the approved pattern, and always ready for inspection by VIPs. Polishing floors, cleaning toilets, showers and washbasins, and stoking and cleaning the large coke stove became second nature and I soon learned that it was much easier to keep out of trouble than to get out of it once in. It was humour that kept us all going during those months and a very cold winter, and we learnt very quickly to lean on each other and become a team. An example of humour occurred on the firing range when we were firing sten guns, a notoriously unreliable weapon given to jamming frequently. One cadet's gun jammed and so he turned round towards the butts where we all were, still pointing his sten gun, calling out,

"Flight Sergeant my gun has jammed." Everyone scattered except for one joker who stood there, calmly took off his helmet and used it to cover his genitals. When loudly questioned by the Flight Sergeant, "What do you think you're doing?", he replied, "I would rather be dead than have this shot off!" The tension dissipated in a flash!

The Sten Guns reminded me of my father during the war; an electrical engineer specialising in industrial metering, his days were spent arranging the repair of bomb damage to essential electrical supplies to coal mines, paper mills, cement works and factories supplying war materials, and at night he became part of the Home Guard and his Sten Gun would always be hanging ready in the cupboard under the stairs except when he was out on duty. We boys never touched it but did look at it longingly. One bonus of my father's connections was that in 1947 he took my brother and me to visit Battersea Power Station when it was very much still generating electricity. We were almost overwhelmed by this huge cathedral buzzing and whirring and it made us feel quite minuscule even though I was already nearly six feet in height. Another visit to industry was made from Cranwell and we were taken to Thoresby colliery (the deepest pit in the UK and quite modern, having been opened in 1925) in Nottinghamshire, and descended the 799m (2596feet) to the coal face to watch the production of coal. Even though much of the work was mechanised by then, it still left me with great admiration and respect for the men who had for so many years worked in far harsher conditions in other older mines.

During the winter leave of 1952 I opted for skiing in Austria which was fun, but the equipment was nothing like that of today – cable bindings and all very sloppy and difficult to control. I did learn one thing namely that I was not very good at skiing, and it was brought home to me as I lay in a hole in the snow having crashed for the umpteenth time, only to have a little local kid flash down the slope to me, circle me twice , confirm that I was still alive before zooming off down and away. How I envied him; he must have been about five or six but had probably been on skis since he was three!

Relaxing after my first solo 18 May 1953

Once into the third term the flying started. First on the Chipmunk, a basic trainer which was very forgiving of the mishandling it often got from ab initio pilots. My first solo was out of Spitalgate on the hills above Grantham but it also was the sad scene when night flying, to watch one of my friends just slowly and gradually fly straight into the ground which of course killed him. I had a grandstand view since I was immediately behind him in the circuit and the feeling of helplessness was almost overpowering. The only other event during my Chipmunk flying was to have a Harvard taxy at quite high speed straight into the front of my stationery aircraft. It was a windy day and difficult to move a light aircraft like a Chipmunk quickly. The impact bent my engine at thirty degrees to the line of the fuselage and although the last Harvard propeller cut was very close to me (2 inches from my right foot) and the starboard fuel tank, I was not injured and there was no fire. The instructor in the Harvard was posted the next day. 2nd June 1953 was the day of Queen Elizabeth II's Coronation. The Officer Cadets from Dartmouth, Cranwell and Sandhurst were tasked with lining the route round Parliament Square. We were bussed up to London from Sandhurst where we were accommodated, which meant a very early start for we were in position by 0800. It was a stressful day with no food or drink for 10 hours (and no toilet either) standing to attention for a lot of the time, sometimes with arms presented, but all in the persistent rain. Soaked to the skin we passed the time watching our shiny bayonets slowly turning to rust. However, it was an honour to be there even though we didn't choose to be, to serve a woman for whom I have the utmost respect both as a person and a Sovereign. Sadly, although I was later to meet a number of members of the Royal family, I never met her.

April 1954 and we moved to the big stuff namely the Balliol T2, the last aircraft designed and built by Boulton Paul.

Balliol T2

I loved it and felt very at home flying it. About the size of or a little bigger than a Hurricane with a Rolls Royce Merlin 35 engine and an eleven and a quarter feet diameter four bladed propeller, power was there for the asking and it was a very forgiving and well-mannered aircraft except for one thing – propeller torque! If you abandoned a landing and started to overshoot putting the power on but did not put a large boot on the rudder pedal at the same time, the aircraft would turn round the propeller and, if you are very near the ground, would perform a very nice but destructive cartwheel. This happened to a close friend of mine who was immediately in front of me on finals to land at Barkston Heath airfield, and I had a grandstand view of the resulting crash. Thank God he was unhurt but the aircraft was a write off. The only minor injury he sustained was a cut on his forehead from when he inadvertently hit himself with his parachute harness! The Balliol had the performance to take us above twenty thousand feet and on a clear night, during cross country flights over the centre of London, we could see all the details of the capital. There was relatively little aerial traffic in those days and no control zones and areas except immediately round airfields. Heathrow didn't exist and Croydon was the main London airport. Lincoln was the main social centre for us although there was little enough time to go girl chasing in the pubs and dance halls. I acquired my first car, a 1929 Riley 9 Monaco with a wood and canvas body which, today would have failed an MOT in every area. It would not do more than 45mph because at that speed the doors flew open from the rickety body and, being rear hinged, acted as large airbrakes!

Amongst all the other activities, I managed to swim a mile a day and got selected for the College swimming team and the waterpolo team. I was never very good at ball games even though my parents and my brother were. So games involving racquets and small balls were not for me although I did play rugby at school and for units I was later posted to, but you could argue that the leather blob used in rugby is not really a ball so it was easier for me! I had started sailing encouraged by a fellow cadet and raced twelve foot national and fourteen-foot international dinghies on the River Trent at Newark, and in 1953 at one regatta on the Gareloch in Scotland we sailed fast Dragon class boats with a crew of three. We didn't do that well in competition but had a lot of fun at the Shandon Hydro, which although restored to its role as a Hotel between the wars, its position next to the deep sea-loch on the Clyde made it essential to the navy once again in 1939. Its popularity declined after WW2 until it was destroyed in 1957 to make way for the Faslane naval base. We also sailed against the RN College Dartmouth, at the mouth of the Dart using their DOD (Dartmouth One Design) dinghies and, wonder of wonders, beat them. Despite that they were very good hosts and we had a very enjoyable time visiting local pubs together.

The physical activities and the flying was balanced by academic instruction for which a mathematical ability and knowledge of Physics was essential. Practical engineering knowledge was provided by making items from raw materials in the workshop and dismantling and reassembling jet engines. All this came in very useful later when I started to work on cars which included Lotus, Ferrari, Mercedes and Volkswagen. Why is it that after reassembly, no matter how meticulous you are, you always fetch up with a small bolt or washer that does not seem to have a home? Being required to write a major thesis was a challenge and something that few, if any of us, had done before, and hours were spent in the library finding necessary data. It was then a matter of getting some kind soul to type it! After my senior term as an Under Officer and the proud bearer of the Queen's Colour on parades, in April 1955 we all graduated and were off to Worksop to fly Meteor 8s, which, apart from one engine failure, was an uneventful time from the flying point of view. I thought the Meteor 8 was a super aircraft and many steps on from the first Meteors I had seen tackling Doodlebugs in 1944 in the skies over Kent. Social life locally was very pleasant and there were some pretty, nice, and fun girls to mix with, and that kept my spirits up. Bless them. Cycling into Worksop with my record player strapped to the carrier was an act of devotion!

Queen's Colour

Meteor 8

In the Front Line

January to July 1956 was spent at RAF Bassingbourn near Royston in Hertfordshire, converting on to the Canberra, initially the T4 trainer and the B2 bomber. Being strategically placed just north of London it was well placed to keep in touch with friends farther north and family down in Kent. By this time, I had graduated to a slightly up market car namely a 1938 Morris 8 Tourer which I bought from my brother. In those days it was perfectly feasible to drive quite quickly from north to south through London, but I could never understand why the car always came to a stop outside Liverpool Street station. The fuel pump contacts would fuse together and the pump stopped working, but it did not take long to learn that a few scientific blows with a spanner would free the contacts and we were on our way again. No need for the AA which I could not have afforded anyway! Having successfully converted to the Canberra, I was posted to No 35 Sqn at RAF Upwood near Ramsey in Rutland in August 1956. This was a main force bomber squadron and these squadrons were the main means of retaliating against any attack from the East. (it was a couple of years before the advent of the 'V' Bombers). Although the aircraft were so much more capable than their WW2 forbears, we were still using basically WW2 plans, equipment, and tactics. One thing we learned was that the Canberra B2 at high altitude at night, in winter, was a very cold place to be, in some ways better than a Lancaster but not much. Social life was very pleasant both on and off the Station, with vicious croquet matches on the lawn in front of the mess which often extended across the road and into the fields beyond. The highlights of flying were the detachments to places like Libya, Malta and Cyprus to drop 1,000lb bombs which were only welcome at very few of the UK ranges. I also upgraded my car to an Austin A40 Somerset, a much more comfortable and stylish car, and more likely to attract the girls! It also had a very useful bench front seat!

Early in 1957 I happened to see a signal asking for volunteers to join No 76 Sqn in Australia engaged in the nuclear testing at Maralinga in South Australia and Christmas Island in the Pacific. Much to my Squadron commander's displeasure I applied and was accepted, for I had always wanted to go to Australia since reading some of Neville Shute's books. In May 1957 I spent the month seconded to 12 Sqn at Binbrook in Lincolnshire converting to the Canberra B6 which was all very sudden since I had only just returned from a detachment to Cyprus and Malta where I had met a rather attractive WREN and this had a significance for later in my life. My visit to Akrotiri in Cyprus was only a short time after the Suez conflict in 1956 in which the French had also been involved, and they were still flying their F84F fighters from Akrotiri which was only half built at that time. It was a steep learning curve for a young pilot during this time. By now I had met the Wren's mother at her flat in St John's Wood and drunk quite a lot of her gin! The girl was still in Malta. Then it was off to OZ where I arrived in July 1957 and started flying in August. The flight out had been in one of the early Comets which the RAF had in service and total elapsed time was less than 24 hours. After arrival I didn't know which way was up or down for that matter, and I had to quickly adapt to a different country, customs, and climate. On August 27 I achieved an ambition and landed at Alice Springs having had a close look at Ayers Rock from the air. Getting used to the 'half past four swill' custom was not difficult when the temperature was around 100deg F, and many pints of beer were rapidly consumed before closing at 6pm! Coober Pedy opal mines proved most interesting with the miners and their families living down in the old mine workings some 30 feet below the surface where it was relatively cooler than the surface. Generators and paraffin fridges made life acceptable and there was a pub to service the small community. All I can remember is the huge mountain of bottles and cans at the back of the pub building!

    I flew various support missions, including at high altitude above 57,000 ft, supporting and training for the sampling missions at Maralinga and Christmas Island, and one tracking mission out of Maralinga on Operation Antler on September 14 but the radiation dose was low. These high-altitude flights were very demanding, the air being thin and the temperatures around minus 85degC. This meant that between the stall and hitting our critical Mach No was about 15 knots and the temperature put severe limitations on the engines thus limiting available power. At that height the sky is black and the curvature of the earth quite pronounced. We had to wear partial pressure suits. Whilst on the Island I carried out a training exercise with HMS Cossack with me in the attack mode to help calibrate their radar. They were most grateful for its realism and that led to a Sunday lunch drinks session on board which was very welcome and went on a bit. I ventured out very carefully on the coral reef surrounding the Island and marvelled at the amazing creatures and colours evident there, and I wished even then that I was a diver and able to take full advantage of it. One thing I remember is the land crabs, which were very large, about 12 inches across the carapace, and with only one enormous claw used for dealing with coconuts. If you accidentally killed one they had a very unpleasant smell. Another habit they had at night was to wander through our two-man tents with their claw vertically erect and scrape it along the underside of our camp beds, and depending on what state we had been in when we went to bed, this would certainly wake us up! One chap adopted a Mantis which spent the day inside his mosquito net and the night on top of it, and existed on a diet of mosquitos and insects.

In November 1957 after Grapple Xray, which I witnessed from the ground with the blast and heat being very impressive even though nearly 30 miles from the burst, I was tasked with flying from the Island to Hawaii with a VIP passenger and a load of very important data to meet up with an RAF transport aircraft on its way back to the UK. Once past the point of no return I lost an engine and had to descend from 47,000 ft to about 25,000 ft. This meant that I was no longer above the weather but had to fly though it on instruments, which was very risky with no storm warning device, and the Intertropical Zone (ITZ) was between us and Hickam AFB. Not an easy or pleasant experience but trying to get the engine fixed did give me ten days in Hawaii, so truly those huge clouds I flew through did have a silver lining, and a party on Waikiki beach with a bunch of Naval nurses from Pearl Harbour made up for all the stress. After that I flew the aircraft back to the Island and then to OZ via Canton Island, Fiji, and Queensland. A three-day stopover in Fiji gave us the opportunity to visit a sugar plantation and the folk there were very hospitable. On the leg from Fiji to Queensland we encountered headwinds which increased our fuel consumption and also met a very large cell of cunim clouds right in our path. From 200 nms away it was obvious that we would have to fly over the top and not round it, so I started cruise climbing up to about 49,000. We traversed it with about 2,000 feet to spare but it took almost an hour to cross it which meant it was around 500 nms across. Those Pacific storms are immense and the anvil would have covered most of the UK. One thing we became quite good at was astro navigation and the aircraft being fitted with a periscopic sextant. Taking shots was very much a team effort and we regularly achieved accuracies of one nautical mile on our fixes. In those days there were few navigation aids across the Pacific and our lives depended on it but it gave us an understanding and great respect for the pioneers who crossed the ocean much lower than us and had to cope with the weather and lack of forecasts and aids. Returning to home in South Australia I was given the choice of staying put or returning to the UK, and since I have to admit that I was at this time feeling a little homesick, I opted for the UK where I arrived back in late December having trundled back on a Hastings transport aircraft which was not the fastest in the world, but was reasonably comfortable and reliable.

Holding

I made my way down to Bearsted near Maidstone which my parents had moved to whilst I was away, and the taxi driver and I had trouble in finding their house, eventually calling at the Manse and asking directions from the Vicar. Since my parents did not know I was coming home they were out at some evening Do and so I had to break into their home and then greet them when they finally returned, having tried the strength of my Father's whisky. A quiet Christmas was probably what I needed after the previous six months of activity and so it was the end of January 1958 before I reported to Coningsby in Lincolnshire to join the Bomber Command Holding Unit to await my next posting. It also gave me time to think a bit about the glamorous WREN I had met in Malta months before. On contacting her mother, and again going and drinking her gin in St John's Wood, I was disappointed to learn that she had returned from Malta some months ago and was now engaged.

The date I remember very well as March 7th for it was suggested that I might like to meet another girl who had also been a WREN in Malta and a friend of her daughter. So, I agreed and drove to South Kensington and was waiting in her flat when this tall, slim, graceful and elegant girl, or rather young woman entered the room. So, I took her out to a Hungarian restaurant in Queensway in the same building as the Pathfinder Club which I frequented. We got along fine but there were not really any sparks between us then. She had left the WRNS and was now a Dental Nurse working for a very upmarket Dentist in Cavendish Square just at the bottom of Harley Street. So back I went to flying in Lincolnshire and it was not until the weekend of the 21st March that I was in London again and called her. Her name was Gillian Farr and we spent that weekend in each other's company with me staying at the RAF Club. I was again in London for the Easter weekend 4th April 1958 and a crowd of us went to Brighton for the day for the weather was fine and sunny, and Gillian had agreed to come with me and we all knew each other so it was fun. Lying in the grass on top of the South Downs looking down at Brighton, I just looked at Gillian sitting beside me and I suddenly knew that this was a relationship that would last and that she was the ONE and if I wanted to keep her then I had better do something about it. To my utter amazement I later learnt that she had realised the same thing but sooner than me. Naturally I took her down to Kent to meet my parents and they approved, although like most mothers, mine was a little nervous at the thought she might be losing a son, but in fact she very much gained a daughter. Of course I also went to see Gillian's mother in Uckfield and ask her permission, which she gladly gave, her father having died some years before. Eight weeks later we were married in Uckfield on 2nd June by a retired Naval chaplain which was very appropriate. We got a lot of support from Gillian's mother, family and friends in Uckfield. So from first meeting to getting married was 12 weeks and 2 days and we were very happily together for over 65 years. The glamorous, now ex WREN was Gillian's bridesmaid. At that time I gave Gillian a promise that if at all humanly possible, wherever I went I would take her with me and the blessing was that I was able to keep that promise.

Wedding June 2nd 1958

Australia

I had opted to return to 76 Sqn in OZ and that left us with the dilemma that I would have to leave less than two weeks after our wedding and, shipping schedules being what they were, Gillian could not arrive until 2nd September. I was also under 25 at the time and therefore would have to pay for her passage. Hence the biblical passage: 'no greater sacrifice has man than he lay down his car and sell it to buy a ship's passage for his wife'. Well perhaps not but being alone in OZ at the start did give me time to get established, buy a car, rent a flat, and make arrangements for Gillian to be met by my Australian friends in case I did not get back in time. The testing on Christmas Island was fairly intensive and, although I trained for it, I did not fly on one of the high-altitude samplers but one of the smaller ones at a height of about 30,000 ft. On August 22nd my crew and I flew on Pennant Shot One and got one of the hottest solid particle samples ever. Our radiation dose (apparently equivalent to 400 chest x-rays all at once!) meant that we could fly no more missions and returned to Australia where I was able to greet Gillian disembarking from the P&O Orsova. She was surprised because she didn't expect me to be there, and I was surprised because at first, I could not see her, but I did see an enormous teddy bear descending backwards down the companionway – Gillian was hidden behind it having won it in a raffle on board. Not surprisingly the reunion was quite emotional. The saddest thing was that within a few weeks of her arrival, her mother unexpectedly died of a brain tumour. My parents, bless them, took over and sorted everything for us since there was so little we could do given the limited travel options available in those days, and the fact that it had happened so suddenly.

After this unwelcome setback, which deprived me of ever getting to know Gillian's mother, we settled down to life in OZ. We made friends in the local community and travelled as much as we could with our limited means (a 1952 Morris Minor convertible) and finances. The car was totally unsuitable for OZ but it took us everywhere, 120 miles for Sunday lunch up country was normal, as was round through Melbourne and the State of Victoria and back down the Murray river. We slept in the car and had to use every available towel and cloth to block the holes round the roof and stop the mozzies getting in. Given that we are both fairly large people, we still do not know how we fitted into that small car. On the way back from the Murray we passed the station of our friends, the Seagers, at Mount Pleasant, to find that they had only just minutes before been hit by a wild fire thanks to some clown tossing a fag end out onto the dry grass verge of the road. We spent the next five hours helping to fight the fire or at least control and minimise its effect. With a fairly stiff breeze blowing this was nigh impossible as the flames leapfrogged over the ground and disappeared into the distance. Fortunately, although the Seagers lost a great deal of their feed and trees they did not lose any of their 5000 sheep, thanks to Joy Seager calling them and the dogs guiding them to safety. We fetched up looking like chimney sweeps! Hal Seager , who then was well in his sixties, was a delightful man with a roguish sense of humour. He had fought at Gallipoli with the Anzacs and the missing back of his skull was evidence of the price he paid!

One thing that was quite noticeable was the number of attractive single women of about 30 that there were. It then hit you that the guys they would have partnered with were those who did not survive WW2 and of which there were many. A look at the register in Lincoln Cathedral of Commonwealth aircrews killed flying from airfields in the Lincoln Diocese alone gives some feel for the high cost in lives. Two of this very group of girls and their mother took us on a trip to NSW and the Snowy Mountains Hydroelectric Scheme, which diverts rivers from flowing into the Pacific, through the mountains and down into the dry centre of the continent. It was very impressive with huge tunnels, massive cathedral-like halls, and huge machines. On exiting the Scheme we got caught in a blizzard, 9 inches of snow in just a few hours. This made driving in the mountains tricky and then when it melted just as quickly, we were cut off for three days by the floods, fortunately stuck in a hotel! These two ladies became long term friends and came to stay with us in the UK on numerous occasions.

Flying in Australia and to New Zealand was interesting and sometimes challenging with the high temperatures and dust storms. I managed to visit most parts of Australia and we had contact with the RAAF; just to the north of Adelaide there was a dirt airfield, Mallalla, which was home to an auxiliary Squadron flying P51D Mustangs and we would act as targets for them at about 10,000 ft. On one such sortie I broke after the Mustang and pulling hard managed to get inside him and he made the mistake of holding the turn. If he had snapped back the other way or done a Derry turn I would not have been able to hold him. The squadron also contributed a formation flypast to the Mallalla open day but three Canberras taking off from a dirt field closed it for quite a time. Once when returning to Adelaide over NSW I gave a routine position report to the station at Wogga Wogga. This was an inflight reporting station and an airfield but you had to give at least an hour's radio warning of landing so that the kangaroos could be cleared off the runway. Our inflight report gave our height as 50,000 ft and the operator asked for confirmation of our height. When confirmed he said, "What the xxxx are you doing up there?" We also used to experiment with different types of landings, simulating undercarriage problems, and it was surprising how far you could get down the runway before having to put the main or nose wheels on the tarmac. This was very useful to me some years later in Germany when I had to do it for real, but that is another story. All good things come to an end eventually and the Squadron returned to the UK in November 1959, based at Upwood and involved in special tasks until mid 1960. We had one aircraft fitted with a 450 gal bomb bay fuel tank which gave an endurance at height of about 8.5 hours, but put its max all up weight near the limit for take-off as I found out on a departure from Idris runway in Libya when it was hot and very bumpy and I only just got off before departing into the desert! Flying over the Sahara about five hundred nautical miles South West of Tripoli at about 5,000 feet I saw a dark spot moving from South West to North East and just sand! Descending to about 500 feet I identified a lone Bedouin trudging through the sand dunes. He didn't react to us but plodded on alone, so camel, no donkey, no companions. So I climbed up to try and see where he had come from and where he might be going. Nothing!! No sign of habitation, life, water, greenery – absolutely nothing. A very interesting area the Sahara, and only the Bedouin know where the buried villages, towns and tracks are, and perhaps more importantly where to find water. The winds often reshape the huge dunes exposing the remains of habitation. That huge area was once thriving with life, and that brings Hanibal's elephants to mind! During this time Gillian had to return to her familiar life pattern with a job and flat in London, and me flying out of an airfield farther north. However, I did manage, courtesy of BEA, to take her out to Malta for two weeks where the Squadron was operating. For her it was familiar territory and she was able to show me all the sights when I was not flying. Otherwise we spent as much time together as we could either in her flat or in a hotel in Ramsey. All I can really remember of that is the huge hotel bath with its naval engineering and plumbing and the fact that it would comfortably hold two people, and probably more if it had been appropriate!

RAF Finningley Yorkshire

I left 76 Sqn at the beginning of June 1960 and attended the OATS Course to give me some admin skills before moving to RAF Finningley as OC General Duties Flight, or General Dogsbody Flight depending how you viewed it. The nearest equivalent would be Station Adjutant with a variety of responsibilities from non-public accounts, serving the needs of the Station Commander, taking parades, arranging duty rosters, and just trying to be useful. There were also interesting areas like grounds, gardens, and vermin control. Surprise, surprise, I also managed to get some flying mainly in the Chipmunk doing glider towing. It was a big and busy station operating Vulcan bombers, but Gillian and I had at last managed to get together again, firstly having a small hiring in Scawsby just outside Doncaster and later we got one of the newly built married quarters which was much better for me. I tried to teach Gillian to drive but it is something that rarely works with married couples, and so I bit the bullet and some BSM lessons did the trick and she became mobile, driving 'Aunt Moss' a 1938 Austin 10! At least she always stood out in a crowd! Our location meant that we had easy access to the Yorkshire Dales and North Yorkshire moors which we loved and walked a great deal in those areas. In 1961 we sailed from Hull to Bergen and toured Norway and Sweden. Instead of sleeping in our Morris Minor Traveller we tented, which neither of us found wholly to our liking possibly because it rained most of the time. We also found that diving bravely into a Norwegian river can be quite a shock since it was June and nothing had yet warmed up. It was however, a beautiful part of the world. One small drawback was the size of the mosquitos which seemed to be near the dimensions of a light aircraft. Whilst at Finningley we used to play squash together and I had to face the regular ignominy of being thoroughly thrashed by Gillian who was very good at both squash and tennis!

2 ATAF Germany

In June 1962 I was posted to 88 Sqn at Wildenrath in Germany to fly Canberra BI8s except that I had to wait until after a Royal Visit by Princess Margaret, and in which I was much involved. So, I was rushed through a Canberra refresher course at Bassingbourn which I completed on 9th July, and during which I met and made a lifelong friend Don Christie also heading for 88 Sqn. In the previous two months I had bought a Lotus Elite sports car intending to do the assembly myself, but my posting changed that and I got it assembled and tax free to take abroad. And so, heavily laden (how much kit can you get in a Lotus even with a roof rack? – to which the answer is quite a lot) we crossed the Channel and made it to Roermond in the Netherlands where we stayed for two weeks, wonderfully looked after by the Dutch, whilst I commuted through the border to Wildenrath and got installed on the station and squadron. No married quarters were available on the station and, not having children and sufficient points, we did not qualify anyway. So, we were offered a quarter down in Koln 53 miles from the station, but it was that or nothing. The house was grand and due to its size (four floors and five bedrooms) soon became known as the Salter Hilton from the number of folks who stayed with us. If I was away during the cold winter months, and the boiler man did not come, Gillian had to declinker a huge boiler (about eight feet in length and nearly five feet high!) and then refill it with between ten and twenty large shovels full of coke. I suppose that was the downside of having such a large house. However, she became an expert stoker and was able to add this to all her other skills. Having the Lotus parked outside 9 Rosburger Str, gave me an introduction to another lifelong friend, an American Bill Orr who was then working on the F104G programme for the Luftwaffe at Norvenich and he also lived in Koln. With his interest in Lotus (he had owned one himself) and cars generally we soon established a close friendship with him and his wife. Indeed we spent a lot of time together travelling all over Europe, and by now he had exchanged his Porsche S90 for a Lotus Elan. We even got to race at the Nurburgring before it was shortened and made safer. That was an experience which Gillian never forgot, to cover 14.5 miles in 12.5 minutes at an average speed of 70 mph on that track was a serious business. At that time there were few cars that could hold a Lotus on a winding road, since it seemed almost as though they were on rails. We even got up to Oslo to visit with Bill's sister and her husband who was in the US Army. If you do not have a head for heights then don't look down the Holmenkollen ski jump! Through Bill we met many other Americans working for the Germans and the Dutch on the F104 programme, and many of them had very challenging cars, ranging from Ferrari, Maserati and the Mercedes 300SL Gullwing which won the Le Man 24 three years running in the mid-fifties driven by Stirling Moss. Mike Bryant the owner lent it to me for three weeks to drive around in, and it was very different to my Lotus, requiring some real muscle power to steer and change gear, but fast and powerful it certainly was.

Canberra BI8

The Canberra BI8 is probably my favourite flying machine and best equates to the Mosquito of WW2. In Germany it had a Nuclear Strike role and conventional capability with bombs and a 4x20mm cannon gun pack which fitted in the bomb bay. Nuclear weapons were delivered using LABS (low altitude bombing system, or Toss Bombing) so we spent most of our time operating at 250 ft agl and things can happen very quickly when you are also travelling at 420 knots. This role also involved QRA (Quick Reaction Alert) which in practical terms meant we had to be armed and airborne within four minutes. There were no allowances for what you might be doing when the klaxon sounded, so you were constantly ready throughout the 24 hours of duty. All you had to do was sprint to the aircraft, climb in, press two buttons to start the engines, and ease the HP cocks forward whilst strapping in, putting your helmet on, and taxying. We proved many times that it could be done. During the bad winter of 1962/63 the aircraft were not covered, and the rain ice meant that the aircrew and groundcrew spent all night getting the sheet ice off the airframe, for they don't fly that well when covered in ice! The conventional role was less scary and more fun, and it is amazing what you can destroy with a 2 second burst from 4x20mm cannons. So there were many detachments to the ranges in North Africa, and further afield to Cypress and Aden. In 1964 we were, at 48 hours' notice, pulled out of Germany and sent to Malaysia to counter President Sukarno of Indonesia's claim to Malaysia and Singapore not to mention Borneo. We went in the conventional role and crossed the Indian Ocean to the Maldives. Sometime after leaving Masirah, off the South coast of Saudi Arabia, I lost a tank fuel pump which made transferring and balancing fuel tricky. It was a choice as to whether we returned to the bare rock and sand of Masirah or carried on to the tropical beauty of Gan in the Maldive islands. My nav George, a Canadian I was crewed with from the start, and I discussed it for about ten seconds and carried on whilst I worked out a way of using the available fuel in sequence. I obviously got it right because it worked and we arrived at this tropical paradise with a safe lagoon for snorkelling, palm trees and sunshine.

What not to like with four days to enjoy it? With the pump replaced we soldiered on via Butterworth, the Australian base in NW Malaysia, and from there crossed to the East coast and landed at our destination – Kuantan a WW2 airfield with only 2,000 yds of concrete runway and a bamboo control tower, everything else was in tents and anything had to be trucked in except fuel which meant we had to fly down to either Tengah or Changi to fill up. Not ideal but necessary and doable. Our task was to fly in at low level and take out the Indonesian airfields and aircraft and George and I worked out our own method for doing so, for we calculated that the official brief for a shallow dive from 1500 ft would mean that we almost certainly would get shot down, and this didn't seem very attractive to either of us. We used China Rock to work it out with live ammunition. Whilst at Kuantan the local chapter of the Red Cross in Kuantan held a big dinner and they very kindly invited us down from the airfield (at least they were grateful for us being there since they did not want to become Indonesians). One of our pilots was named John Hanson and he found himself sitting next to a tall blond guy and so he introduced himself. The guy took his hand and said, "I am also Jon Hansen," and he was, a Dane running a rubber plantation up near the Thai border. We got directions and 'visited' him by air on a training mission later that week. George, my nav, was a character and a very good navigator so we got along fine. As a youngster he had lied about his age and fought in Korea and the scars from a grenade in his back proved it! He had also been on the bare-knuckle prize fighting circuit at Canadian Rodeos and been in the RCAF flying CF100 all-weather fighters.

In 1961 he and his family had crossed the pond and he had joined the RAF. He was also a parachutist and had been in the RCAF sky diving team. We shared many realistic views of the world and trusted each other professionally. Sadly, he was killed in the crash of a Hastings transport aircraft at Abingdon in March 1965.

By early December 1964 we were back in Germany the Indonesian bubble having been burst. Whilst taking off from Wildenrath on 21st December the tower called and said "We think something fell off your aircraft and we think it was a nosewheel." My reaction was immediate and the undercarriage clunked down. An inspection from the tower confirmed that one nosewheel had come off and was eventually retrieved, and the other one was hanging precariously on the end of the axle. To me this meant spending a lot of time burning off fuel and getting the balance aft so that I would be able to keep the nose up for as long as possible after landing. All those hours in Australia spent working this out started to pay off. So, two hours later I put the aircraft down on a foam strip, kept the nose up and the result was no damage to the aircraft and only an inch ground off the bottom of the nosewheel leg casting. Cause: it had been serviced and whoever did it failed to lock the nuts holding the whole assembly together and the take-off run had undone them.

No 1 ITS South Cerney Glos

To be posted back to the UK and the No 1 ITS at South Cerney initially seemed something of a backward step but in reality turned out to be a challenge and I found a knack for teaching having taken over the Foreign Nationals training flight with students from Jordan and Saudi Arabia. I looked at the teaching syllabus, which to me seemed wholly inappropriate for foreign students to have to learn how an English officer's mess runs, and I completely changed the teaching to concentrate on those subjects the students would have to cope with once they joined a Flying Training School. As one of our educators put it: "You can tell these guys what a spanner is , but you don't need a spanner to service a camel!" This was in no way derogatory since in their youth these boys had not played with bicycles or messed with machinery and cars, so many things that were second nature to us were completely foreign to them, and the higher the social level they came from the worse the problem was. Physics and how weather developed was completely strange to them. The proof that these changes worked, came some years later when I was at Farnborough and a foreign officer came up to me, introduced himself as one of my former Saudi students, and thanked me for what I had done to help them get through flying school.

Initially we lived in a rental house in Chedworth, a typical Cotswold village to the north of Cirencester. Part of the 'Old Forge' was listed as 15th century and the draughts coming through the walls confirmed this! The house was strategically placed within a short distance of both the Church and the Pub; I forget which one we spent most time in. It was an interesting first winter in the Cotswolds, and made especially so when Bill Orr, my friend from Germany days with his family of wife and four kids, turned up, stayed with us and eventually rented a house over in Syde just to the west of us and stayed there for about nine months before returning to the US. This gave us all an introduction into the local Cotswold community, mainly farming, and this was very informative and fun. We all became great friends with the Whitaker family who had farmed in Syde for many years and still do, although Malcolm and his wife have since passed on. After some seven months or so we were offered and accepted a married quarter on the station which meant no more commuting. In 1967 I developed mumps and fetched up with every complication in the book, and spent so I am told, three days in an ice bath to keep my temperature down. Gillian had also got sick at the same time so our convalescence was together for three weeks in our caravan in South Devon during a beautifully sunny summer.

A colleague on the staff of the ITS was involved in sub-aqua diving, and persuaded me to give it a try in the old quarry lakes in the area. I was hooked, and it became my main hobby even surpassing my interest in cars. Having joined the BSAC (British Sub Aqua Club) I did as much diving as I could and eventually trained and became qualified as an instructor. This meant that I could legitimately take over the running of any club in the future. Our expeditions were to Cornwall around Looe and Devon in the Plymouth area where I was able to dive on the 'James Egan Lane' a Liberty ship torpedoed in the Channel in 1944 and eventually sank in Whitsand Bay. Being in those days virtually intact with the mast still standing and just sitting on the sandy bottom, it was an ideal dive site, but you had to plan carefully for it would have been easy to get snagged and trapped within the hull, and you never went alone.

In late 1968 we crossed the Atlantic in a Panam DC8 to go and stay with Bill Orr and his family now living near Annapolis, MD. The flight from London went via Philadelphia to Baltimore, out destination. From PA to MD we were the only passengers on the plane and were invited up to flight deck, (since they knew I was a pilot) to meet the crew, and the rest of the trip we sat with the hostesses drinking coffee. I cannot imagine that happening today! We had a very pleasant if cold stay before catching an RAF Britannia flight out of Andrews AFB and back to the UK.

22 Squadron RAF St Mawgan Cornwall

Towards the end of my time at South Cerney I felt like a complete change and opted to move to helicopters. With hindsight it seems almost perverse to move from heights around 50,000 ft to heights around 50ft! But it proved to be a smart and challenging move and I was promoted to Squadron Leader and in 1968 given command of No 22 Sqn, a search and rescue unit. There were two such sqns, 22 covering the West and South coasts of the England, and 202 covering the east coast and Scotland. Our main task was supposed to be the rescue of downed aircrew on land or at sea, but probably 90% of the work was civilian, ship disasters, injured climbers and walkers, yachts in trouble, in fact anything requiring rescue by helicopter. This could include transporting serious road accident casualties to hospital and moving medical staff around, something now done by Air Ambulances and the Coast Guard. We were somewhat limited by the helicopter we had – the Whirlwind Mk 10. Originally the Sikorsky H19 with a radial piston engine, even re-equipped with a Rolls Royce Gnome Turbine engine, power was always limited. The other problem with the Whirlwind was that it had no auto-stabilisation or auto pilot, and the pilot could not take his hands off the controls. Of course, we all learnt the tricks of the trade even down to flying it with your knees! It always gave me the greatest pleasure to write citations for awards when crews had gone above and beyond what seemed the possible to effect a rescue. They had operated themselves and their aircraft right at the edge of the envelope and sometimes outside it! The NATO nations took turns in organising and holding a Search and Rescue Helicopter meet with realistic competitions and this gave me the opportunity to fly other types such as Kaman HH43 Husky a most unusual design, and the Sikorsky H34 operated by the Belgians in the SAR role, and this was the basic airframe of the Wessex. On 18th October 1968 I was tasked with flying due West from St Mawgan to 06.30deg W to pick up an injured crewman from an Oberon class submarine Aird Whyte which took me almost due south of Cork in Ireland. It was a difficult mission for a number of reasons: at the limit of our radius of action, a very short available time on task due to fuel restrictions, and increased weight for we had to carry a dinghy. Once on task the wind was across the Atlantic swell that was rolling the sub around making the conning tower very difficult to hover over, but we did the job and got the guy back to base and into an ambulance. We did not, however, have enough fuel to deliver him direct to hospital.

Whirlwind MK10

22 Sqn was spread down the West coast of England and Wales, with flights at Valley in Anglesey, Chivenor in north Devon, Headquarters at St

Mawgan Newquay Cornwall, Thorney Island in Hampshire, and Manston in Kent. Manston had particular memories for me since in 1947 my parents took my brother and me with them when they played a tennis match against the Americans who were operating their F84s from there. After the match we were all entertained royally and given long unavailable things like ice cream, what luxury! After eating, there was dancing for the adults, and it was the first time I had seen couples jiving. The music was great since I was by then a Glen Miller fan having first heard his orchestra on the radio in 1943 when they arrived in the UK prior to D Day, but the dancing was an eye opener and unbelievably athletic. It was amazing just where the girls got to! Being stationed at St Mawgan meant that the whole of the South West was available for diving and the station club took advantage of our good fortune. In the late sixties there were few restrictions on where you could dive or launch an inflatable. We made it our business to be disciplined, obey the commonsense and wildlife rules, and cultivate good relations with the fishing community by retrieving lost objects for them, and of course we already had good working relations with the Police and Coastguard. We also got involved in marine surveys and I fetched up helping David Bellamy with cup coral studies for Durham University. I also managed to persuade my superiors that it would be to every one's advantage if I were to complete the Royal Navy Diving course, and so from mid-February to mid-March 1969 I was at HMS Drake in Plymouth at the coldest time of the year, and spent a total of 15.5 hours underwater doing lots of challenging and interesting things, including ship's bottom searches at night, underwater welding, and using different types of diving equipment, not to mention jumping off a 30ft high ship's deck and doing the mudrun. A very tough but enjoyable 4 weeks which I took out of my annual leave. I also was co-leader of an Archaeological diving expedition to Gibraltar where ship remains had been uncovered during work on the dock walls. We recovered many artefacts for the local museum and the ships proved to be hulks that had been used as fire weapons against the Spanish 300 years before.

I had one significant incident with a Whirlwind when transiting from St Mawgan to Culdrose to deliver a spare to a stranded Shackleton. I was flying solo having just completed a training session of engine off landings, and when about 20 nms from Culdrose at a height of 700 ft agl, I suffered an explosion and fire in the engine bay. With hindsight I must have reacted very quickly because I made a distress call, went through the emergency procedures and checks, before the dense toxic smoke from burning electric cable insulation, prevented me from seeing anything, inside or outside the cockpit. From then on all I could do was freeze on the controls and hope I was keeping the helicopter upright as I autorotated down. After what seemed an age the smoke cleared enough for me to see the ground and identify what I thought were cattle, then a stone wall appeared which I hopped over and plonked it down having flared off the speed, only to then see the low poles carrying high voltage cables right in front of me. It was the main electrical supply to Falmouth dockyard. The brakes on the Whirlwind were not the best and I just managed to stop a few feet before the rotor blades would have hit the cables. That, with all the fuel swilling about would have been quite a funeral pyre! I worked it out that the time from the explosion to being on the ground was less than 20 secs and I found that the cattle were in fact pigs, so I was a lot lower than I thought. I was picked up by a Culdrose helo and delivered the Shackleton spare. A team came down from 22 Sqn HQ and repaired the helicopter wiring and the snapped fuel filter clamp which had caused the trouble, and I later that afternoon flew it manually back to St Mawgan where it took slightly longer to repair the damage which included structural metal that had been burnt through. I had landed on one of the few flat pieces of ground in Cornwall and it happened on the same day November 1st 1968 as the Scillie Islands helicopter crashed in what was, fortunately, shallow water and an RN Wessex had gone in on the side of a hill in Cornwall. A very busy day for Culdrose!

India

My next posting in 1970 was very different and unexpected: Assistant Air Adviser in the British High Commission in New Delhi India. It took about 4 months to complete all the training, briefings, and obtaining the right uniforms, clothing and household items. As usual Gillian was an absolute star in all this, but commuting from Cornwall to London and other areas for briefings was a bit tedious. Finally we were ready, climbed in our heavily laden old Mercedes and drove to Trieste to board a Lloyd Triestino ship bound for Bombay round the Cape, calling at various ports en route including Venice, Capetown, Durban (where we met up with some friends of my mother's), Mombasa (which meant we were able to visit the Tsavo game park) and then across the Indian Ocean to Bombay. This was the way the Foreign Office did things in those days and it was very useful in that we made friends onboard whom we were to have contact with later. It always struck me as a high-risk venture since all our worldly wealth and belongings were with us including the car with overloaded roof rack! We made it to Bombay without incident and, to our amazement, all our goods eventually arrived in Delhi intact. I was trained to use a camera professionally and this gave my latent interest in photography a big boost, and during this time I equipped myself with an array of Nikon equipment which came in useful there and until I later graduated to digital cameras. The only problem it creates is, "What to do with all the photographs?" Later in 2004 I bit the bullet and digitised hundreds of them and they are safely stored on my computers, although I seem to have lost a lot over the years.

The culture shock was marked but we had good briefings from colleagues and, I found myself working for Group Captain John Forbes who, with his wife Wendy was most kind and helpful. Needless to say they became great friends until way after we both retired. Gillian and I decided early on that it was important to make contacts and friends in the local community, particularly if you wanted to really understand the country and its people. Fortunately, the common language both north and south was English, there being many regional tongues and dialects and the Indians themselves did not understand one another. One thing difficult to get used to at first was the number of people, in fact it was impossible to be alone, even on a picnic in the country. You would stop in an apparently deserted area, but within minutes there would be a ring of faces watching you, a mixture of humans and animals. We quickly made friends in Delhi, Bombay, Kerala and the Nilgiris which is tea country, and joining the Royal Bombay Yacht Club not only gave access to sailing but also many Indian contacts in Bombay (now Mumbai). Since at that time the Indian military were half trained and equipped by the Soviets and the other half by the West, there was a great deal of intelligence interest which kept me occupied, even down in Bombay harbour. (Photographing Russian equipment was routine and one developed methods for doing this without attracting attention). Sailing the local Seagull design yachts, 18ft third decked and gunter rigged, was great fun and both the sea/river waves and winds were challenging. Dear Gillian was always there with me and was a great companion, and a good rope puller!

Taj Mahal

    We arranged excursions for ourselves, such as Corbett wildlife park where we viewed elephants trotting along at about 30mph almost silently, and mounted safely on the back of one viewing tigers in the wild crossing the track ahead of us, and Simla and the inevitable tourist triangle: Agra, Jaipur, Delhi Red Fort. It was most impressive to watch an elephant rolling an egg around on the ground with its foot. Not so impressive was to have the elephant in front , or the one on which you were seated, have an attack of flatulence, firstly because the noise would have scared off all wildlife within miles of us and the smell would have cleared the Albert Hall in a flash. I was taken officially by the Indian authorities to parts that are not normally open to ordinary travellers. At high altitude in Sikkim we could look across the border at the Chinese military and listen to their blaring loudspeakers pumping out propaganda and martial music. I had a responsibility for the function of the Gurkha repat route between the garrison in Hong Kong and Nepal, and was involved in negotiations with the Indian authorities to make the passage of Gurkhas and their families returning to Nepal as trouble free as possible. I visited Nepal on two occasions. One at the invitation of the Gurkha HQ and the other to take a diplomatic bag and bring another back from the British Consulate there. I did however get a sunset view of Everest not that far away and another at dawn, both very impressive. A visit to a girls orphanage near Darjeeling allowed us to see the amazingly fine work they did embroidering silk pictures, which look almost like paintings. We became friends with a Sikh family, and their farm outside Delhi was a gathering place for many nationalities and a number of useful contacts and lasting friendships were made there. Gillian and I travelled widely, by road if we could, but managed to visit Calcutta, Goa, Madras, Cochin, Bangalore and many other places in between. I had a three day voyage from Cochin to Goa in a RN minehunter which, by nature of its role, had a team of RN divers on board and, as soon as they knew that I was a qualified RN diver, took me under their wing and I was invited to the Senior Rates' Mess for 'refreshments' which was great fun and a privilege.

There were a number of unusual events in which I became involved: in the early morning of 24th June 1972 JAL 471 from Thailand to Delhi, crashed well short of the runway and impacted the steep bank of the River Jumna. It piled the wreckage up and the fire destroyed everything and everyone. One little Swedish girl was thrown clear and survived, but what impact it would have had on her emotionally can only be imagined. I got involved with the High Commission doctor (a British Army officer) and we helped look after the consular issues relating to the British passengers on board. This involved inspecting bodies in a make shift morgue, a schoolroom with large blocks of ice to keep the temperature down, and the burnt bodies laid out in lines. Such a sad sight and not a pleasant smell! I also visited Hong Kong on the way back from the UK in order to consult the Gurkha Battalion HQ there, about the repat route for Gurkhas through India. I also was casevaced to Changi Hospital in Singapore because of very persistent stomach parasites a problem I had first encountered transiting Pakistan in 1958. Not so nice but it did give me the opportunity to meet the Chinese merchant who supplied the Delhi High Commission with any goods on a personal basis and I was the agent who arranged all this. It was a great honour to unexpectedly be taken out to dinner by him and his family before I left the hospital and flew back to India via Bangkok. We naturally had servants at home and our cook, a Gurkha called Bahadur, lived with his family in the servant's quarters beyond the garage. We made it a rule that none of those who worked for us would go to money lenders, which was to enter a lifetime of debt. If they needed help they came to me. So, in our second year there Bahadur's daughter got married and the wedding was held on our front lawn with much of the trimmings for it supplied by us. This saved him a fortune and gave us an opportunity to witness, and be part of, a Hindu wedding.

MOD One

Returning to the UK in May 1973 I took up a post in MOD Flight Safety and this proved to be interesting and rewarding, although the commuting, first from Bushey Heath where we were given a Married Quarter and later from Farnham in Surrey where we bought our first house, was a bit of a shock. Organising International Flight Safety conferences proved to be something of a challenge, but the job itself involved airfield ground maintenance working with MAF and statistical work, including answering Parliamentary Questions, which always seemed to arrive at about 4pm on a Friday which was far from convenient when the answer was wanted almost by return! There was also a concern about birds, especially those that tended to flock like lapwings and gulls which, when they did so on or near an airfield became a threat to aircraft from bird strikes. I was on a bird related visit to RAF Valley in 1974 when my father died suddenly and I had to take the night train south to get to Kent to be with my mother, since my brother at that time was working in East Africa where he was the Shell Operations Manager. It was an emotional shock having to deal with all the admin surrounding a death, although it was much simpler in those days than it is now. Since my father collapsed mowing the lawn, it was good for him but much more of a shock for my mother, whom we had to try and console. I was able to take up diving again and there were regular weekend commutes from Surrey to Plymouth and the diving centre at Bovisand. I was also able to pick up again with some of my naval friends made during the RN diving course. Sadly, I had to stop diving in 1975 because of ear trouble which would have prevented me from flying. In all I calculated that over my diving years I had spent 75 hours under water which I thought was not too bad for a hobby. Faithful Gillian was to be seen waiting on cold quaysides or bobbing about in diving boats waiting for me to appear from below. She always had her binoculars handy and spent the time usefully bird watching. We also visited the Farne Islands where I met a grey seal coming round a rock face and it was just as startled as I was but I did manage to take its picture since I had an underwater Nikon camera. Gillian and I were both bird watchers but not 'twitchers' and the Farne Islands were a magnificent place for viewing some of the nicer and more interesting sea birds (like Kittiwakes), other than obnoxious herring gulls!

72 Sqn RAF Odiham Hants

1975/6 was spent at the Joint Services Staff Collage then at Latimer with the prospect of promotion to Wing Commander and command of another helicopter squadron, and in November 1976 I took command of 72 Sqn at RAF Odiham flying the Wessex MK2. This was the start of the busiest two years of my career with one of the largest totally mobile squadrons in the RAF with a parish from Northern Ireland to the Iron Curtain. With a permanent detachment at RAF Aldergrove NI, I spent many weeks flying as a squadron pilot in NI during the troubles, and the flying there was very challenging especially at night using the first generation Night Vision Goggles. It started with a rush and in January 1977 I was initiated into basic operating in the field with a detachment to Catterick for troop exercises but, because it became a very harsh winter in the North, it morphed into flying animal feed to stranded cattle and sheep in the Otterburn area of Northumberland. We were sleeping and living in the helicopters and it was very cold, so it seemed more like living in a cold store! Very soon after that in February it was off to Northern Ireland to learn the ropes there and fly as an ordinary squadron pilot for three weeks on operations mainly out of Bessbrook. This gave me a very deep baptism into what the guys did during their six-week detachments to the Province. It was exciting but very demanding and tiring with non-stop operating. I spent a total of 12 weeks flying in NI during my time with 72 and made 6 trips to Germany for exercises and liaison with 18 sqn, for there was a close association with 18 sqn for we had many shared assets and interests. We were able to stay in our house in Farnham which was just a few minutes from Odiham, and this was very much better for entertaining the guys and their wives and was much more personal than a married quarter. Curiously the house Number was '72'! Two events stand out in my memory: Odiham hosted a reunion of SOE (Special Operations Executive) agents most of whom had flown to the continent from Odiham during WW2 and it was great honour to talk to these incredibly brave people, Danes, Norwegians, Dutch, French, and English, all of whom had remarkable stories to tell; Odiham also hosted the boys from Treloar School in Alton for a wheelchair marathon, with which I assisted and I was so impressed with them, that I arranged with my Station Commander that we should fly the six winners back from Odiham to their school, and these photos record the event on 8 June 1978.

Wessex Mk2: me checking oil levels

The Squadron had 300 personnel assigned to it, 24 helicopters, 50 vehicles ranging from Hiab trucks to bowsers, Land Rovers and even motorcycles. We went where the army went, supporting them in the field, and all we needed was fuel, water and food. We defended ourselves, thanks to an RAF regiment team, and had our own domestic facilities, and it is quite surprising how quickly you grow to tolerate or even like compo rations. QRA (quick reaction alert) required that we generate our assets and have them on their way to somewhere in Europe within a few hours. Some assets would leave almost immediately with the others to catch up later. We would find ourselves in some forest such as in Denmark, which was populated by wood mice and a lot of them. They were pretty little creatures quite unlike the house mice we have here. However, I did have two things against them, their liking for dancing on my mess tin and waking me up in the middle of the night, and nicking my chocolate bar hidden in my nav bag. It was at this time that two of our helicopters , and I was piloting one, climbed to 10,000 feet over Copenhagen to drop a team of British Army parachutists who would be aiming at a school playground during some celebration there. The guys on the Squadron, both air and ground crews worked very hard and spent a lot of time away from home due to the permanent detachment in Northern Ireland, but at any time in the year there would also be at least two other helos and crews away somewhere on exercise. It was a very busy time for all of us for the Cold War was still going strong. Towards the end of my time with 72 we were on detachment in Germany hidden in a beech forest. It was October 1978, and the weather was tricky with fog and bad visibility. On the day of our planned departure for home to the UK we were given a quite reasonable weather forecast so my 4-ship formation took off with the intention of staging through Wildenrath where we updated the weather forecast, refuelled and took off for Manston. Our helos were heavily laden with equipment and passengers who preferred air travel to a long bumpy trip home by road in a truck. Very soon we sensed that something was not quite right, and started working the radios to check on the weather since it was getting more and more difficult to see the ground. By the time we were over Belgium we could see virtually nothing of the ground and had no radio contact on any of our three radios and it wasn't just my radios because all 4 crews were trying. It wasn't until the Channel coast that we managed to raise Manston only to learn that the whole of NW Europe was out in thick fog. By now we were getting tight on fuel and very concerned about what to do. At least with a helo, if you can see at least a little of the ground you have a chance to get it down somewhere, but that would be the last resort. Further enquiries established that the only airfield within range that was still open was Gatwick but that would be another 30 mins to run. It was going to be very, very tight, and I could see my career going up in smoke! I contacted Gatwick, explained our predicament and declared an emergency PAN. We were given a priority approach straight in and with a chorus of sighs of relief we landed and were parked in a dispersal just to the North of the main runway. Within 20 minutes, the runway had completely disappeared in fog, it was that close. When refuelled all 4 helos took the maximum tank capacity so we must have all been running on fumes! Thank God for small mercies since I was off to the USA within a matter of days.

America

November 1978 saw us off to the US to take a post in the British Defence Staff which was part of the British Embassy in Massachusets Avenue, Washington DC. We had to find a house and then furnish it, then get our boxes, unpack and establish ourselves in a new and strange country. Fortunately language was not a problem and additionally our friends the Orrs had returned home by this time and were there to greet us. Packing and unpacking our worldly goods was always an interesting exercise, and one which inevitably fell on Gillian. She always insisted on doing the packing of the boxes and to her everlasting credit, in all our moves nothing was ever broken! We found a townhouse in Mclean VA which we liked and it was in a quite large community which meant we were able to make local contacts. Supermarkets and boutique shops were a short distance away in Mclean village, and large shopping mall complexes were within easy reach. What really pleased us was how relatively cheap everything was, from food to clothes, to electricals and anything automotive. Being walkers we found that this was a luxury we could not enjoy as we could at home, and cars were essential even for very short journeys. So biting the bullet we bought two Fords, the first and last Fords I have ever owned. A Galaxy quite unlike its British cousin had a 5.3 ltr V8 engine, very large but with no more interior space than my Volvo at home, and a Pinto of bursting into flames fame! Fortunately, ours never did and took us all the way up through New England to Nova Scotia, and back down the St Lawrence River to Montreal and then South through New York state and home, following the fall colours all the way.

Jefferson Memorial Washington DC

My job, amongst other things gave me responsibility for RAF officers on exchange tours with the Americans, either USAF or US Marines. They were spread throughout the country from coast to coast, and in 1979 in the midst of the fuel crisis, Gillian and I made a road trip half duty and half leave, and visited these guys, their families and their units which also gave me the opportunity to fly in some interesting aircraft and helicopters. One highlight was to spend nearly two hours in a Pave Low equipped CH53H, at night, at heights below 150ft in the mountains North of Alburquerque NM. It was very hard and skilled work for the crew, but an amazing capability for doing night rescues. Flights in US Army Chinooks were fairly routine and of interest since the RAF was just about to take delivery of them. It was also of great interest to do a complete survey of a Galaxy C5 transport and marvel at the carrying capacity. The tail boom, the sole purpose of which is to carry the controls to the tailplane, was bigger than the cargo hold of a C130 Hercules transport aircraft which is fairly big in its own right! Whilst in CA we went to Monterey Bay and visited Cannery Row, or what was left of it, made famous by John Steinbeck. In the bay were sea otters, very appealing creatures.

My other job was to arrange and monitor UK contributions to US Air Shows and the organisers of these show were always asking for the Red Arrows and the Vulcan bomber. Being at these shows gave me many opportunities to meet people from all over the country and especially the 'War Birds' those enthusiasts maintaining and flying historic aircraft. There was great enthusiasm in the US for all things aviation. Two of these shows, Cleveland and Chicago, were relatively easy and quick to get to either by air or by road, and Gillian and I attended them a number of times. We met such people as John Glenn the astronaut, who at that time was a Senator for Ohio, and a pleasant and modest man. At the first Cleveland show we went to, we were seated at a table for dinner and there was one empty seat later filled by Bill Clark who had flown in from State College, PA in his Mustang P51D 'Dolly'. We made instant friends with him and his wife Julia, and it later became a lasting relationship with visits across the Atlantic, and in the UK I was later able to fly him around in my shared Bolkow 208 to Old Warden and the museum at Duxford. We also made a few trips to airfields where, in obscure hangars, upwards of fifteen

Spitfires and one Me109 were being either rebuilt or restored, a long labour of love. What happens when the guys with all these technical skills are no longer with us I don't know.

Mount Rushmore SD

At the suggestion of the Orrs we tried skiing, which was easily done in the US. However, neither of us fancied kami kaze skiing and opted for cross country skiing. To do this successfully and at altitudes above 10000ft you needed to be fit. Since I had started jogging, joining the Washington DC lunchtime jogger mob, and I had become fitter than I had ever been, skiing in Yellowstone Park (manoeuvring round the buffalos and keeping a watchful eye open for bears) and being able to claim that we skied Chicago when it dumped 10ft of snow on the area, were unusual and very pleasant experiences and also challenging. One highlight for me was at New Year's late at night in the moonlight and the snow, to jog into Yellowstone to the hot springs area and marvel. I now know what a Rocky Mountain High really is, and it has nothing to do with drugs! The thing about Cross country skiing is that, providing there is sufficient snow, you can ski anywhere, even uphill! We were in Snowbird ski resort in Utah north of Salt Lake City , when a guy appeared from the north with his dog, and a pack on his back, Nordic touring skis on his boots, and thus the ability to go anywhere. He had made about 60 miles down the mountain ridge over three or four days camping out. That was impressive because he must have skied through some deep snow and faced the risk of avalanches too. But what freedom!

The inevitable trip down South took us firstly to Florida and the Everglades where my cameras worked overtimes to capture everything. There were the crocs, avoided with care, and numerous encounters with racoons, those masters of highway robbery, and they always get away with it because they look so appealing. However, they need to treated with great respect for if frightened or angered they can be quite understandably nasty to self-protect as they see it. In my efforts to get pictures of mangroves I found that the Everglade mosquitos have the ability to easily bite through denims and my backside looked as though I had measles by the time they had finished. On the way out of the Park a few days later we and others in our vehicles were ambushed by a racoon standing in the middle of the road with its hands up and it, and its friends who all appeared from the bushes at the side of the road, were not satisfied until they had all been fed. Then we were released to continue our journey.

We had a three-week holiday trip to North Carolina renting a lodge near the Appalachian trail and Smoky Mountains Park. We tried the trail and walked about 17 miles in all and having got up early we passed the black bear families and manoeuvred round the black snakes and copperheads, who were still very sleepy since it was early morning and we had been up and out since 5.30. On another day there we came across a very attractive river, with large rocks and a healthy flow of water. I wanted to take a photo upstream and stood on a rock mid-stream with my monopod and camera taking the picture I wanted. That is where the Monarch butterflies found me and I became covered in butterflies tickling my skin. It was not a sign of affection on their part, but an interest in the salt in my sweat since it was June and I had my shirt off. Whilst we were there in NC my birthday came by again and Gillian asked me what I would like to do. I had in my wallet a letter of introduction to the Jack Daniels Distillery which was over in Tennessee. That would be a 500-mile round trip, and we discussed whether it was feasible and concluded that it was doable. Since JD was my tipple and had been for many years and it was my birthday, we bit the bullet and went. It was a long trip since not that much was on the interstates. So, we arrived in Lynchburg TE and were welcomed at the distillery and did the tour. We were invited to the JD hospitality house downtown Lynchburg and given a magnificent southern lunch served on long trestle tables with guests on either side and a host/hostess at the end. We soon realised that the folk opposite us were English and we started talking only to find out they were visiting a son who worked in Houston in Texas, and that they lived in Surrey. Where? Farnham our home town too, what are the chances of that happening? Only one downside to the visit is that Lunchburg is in a dry county so no tipples. If you want to drink or buy Jack Daniels you go to the nearest wet county! A smart move on the part of JD himself for they must have saved a fortune not giving out free samples! I also learnt that the oak barrels that JD made for their own whisky, once used were shipped to Scotland for the distilleries there, although I do not know if that continues.

On a trip to the Eastern Shore of MD in the early fall, we were visiting the wildlife sanctuary at Assateague and viewing a large lake which seemed to be completely full of snow geese when a flight came from the North (I estimated about five hundred snow geese), and with two circuits and a few honks, all landed safely on this already crowded lake. No collisions, no squabbles, just brilliant control. All these birds were making their annual migration South from Canada.

MOD Two

Despite our love of America, all good things come to an end eventually, and so back to the UK in November 1981. First priority was to restore our house after a three year occupancy by chain smokers. Never again would we make that mistake! Second priority was to unpack, get the skis out, and take advantage of a big dump of snow in the Farnham area soon after we got back. It was good to catch up with family and friends, but we found the prices of everything took our breath away at first. With accumulated leave, plus the Christmas period, I did not report to my new job in MOD until January 1982 where I took over the Helicopter Desk in ACAS Ops empire at a time when we were trying to plan for the introduction of the Chinook into RAF service. So I tried to get to grips with this, both the concept and the costs, and I had not got far when we were forced into the Falklands war by the Argentinian invasion and I found myself doing my desk job helping to prepare the loading of ships during the day and, on a rota basis, writing intelligence briefs for the Chiefs of Staff at night. This meant long days and nights during those tense months but it was the same for everyone and we all had our troops in the Falklands very much at heart, especially after the 'Atlantic Conveyor' was sunk taking all the helicopters and spares packs with her, and leaving one lone Chinook to support our ground forces. It says a great deal about the crew that flew it and the groundcrews who kept it going with no equipment or spares, the dramas they went through is another story, but they never failed to respond to the ground troops' needs, operating way outside limits and breaking many rules just to get the job done. As I was now getting nearer to the end of my career, it was obvious that flying jobs and flying in the RAF would become less available to me. So I started training at Blackbushe to get a civil licence and succeeded getting a PPL and instrument flying endorsement. I also joined the Tiger Club, then operating out of Redhill aerodrome, and was able to fly many different types from Tiger Moth to a Turbulent, an open cockpit utility aircraft powered by a VW engine! I also bought a share in a Bolkow 208C and was able to use this for trips away. Gillian flew with me on many occasions and I whilst on 72 Sqn I had also been able to take her up (quite legally) in a Wessex. This is us just about to depart from RAF St Mawgan after spending a weekend there in 1983 with the Station Commander who was a friend.

RAF Aldergrove and Northern Ireland

In November 1982 I was sent to RAF Shawbury for a Wessex refresher before being promoted to Group Captain and sent to command RAF Aldergrove in Northern Ireland, and appointed as Senior RAF Officer NI, which is a long winded way of saying that my predecessors and I, were responsible for all the RAF in NI. I was also Air Adviser to the GOC, to the Secretary of State for NI, and responsible to C-in-C Strike Command, AOC 1 Group, Air Officer Scotland and NI, for the RAF assets in NI. By now 72 Sqn were permanently in situ there with families and committed solely to the OPS in NI and no detachments elsewhere, and this meant that I was able to fly operationally with them and at least keep my hand in, so together with flying the Bulldogs of Queen's University Air Squadron, I had access to the air! It was a very busy time with many VIP visits including Royalty, Prime Minister, Secretary of State, and many senior civil and service people who needed briefing on the situation in NI, and all this was a long time before Good Friday Agreements so the conflict was very much ongoing. Social life was very busy both on the camp and outside and we enjoyed the company and humour of our Irish friends. Margaret Murphy was an artist friend we particularly valued and admired her paintings of water and the rich colouring of Irish bogs, her use of colour and light were outstanding. Surprisingly she liked my photographs of similar subjects, so we were able to exchange gifts. However, we did buy a number of her paintings since we liked them so much. Gillian went off to Donegal (in the Republic) with her on a painting trip.

I managed to continue keeping fit by jogging around the camp area within the security fence. It was not considered safe for us to go outside the camp alone and always had members of our security team with us. This could be very useful in that I did not have to drive but sit in state in the back whilst being chauffered around. It also produced slightly amusing situations such as during my taking Gillian out to dinner for our 25th wedding anniversary, there were two inconspicuous guys over the far side of the restaurant with bags at their feet of a slightly strange shape. They were a very good bunch, most helpful and always sensitive to the current situation, such as me taking the salute for a parade in the High Street of Armagh, not long after it had been bombed with disastrous and fatal results. This sort of event was offset by others, such as floating on Strangford Lough eating oysters and drinking Guinness, in the sunshine too which was a plus for Ireland! In 1984, partly for nostalgic reasons I had bought another oboe, not quite the quality of the one I had the loan of thirty years before. It took me about a year to get it up to the playing standard I wanted which included a spell with a specialist company in London, and the help of a member of the Green Jackets Band. But I really got some personal satisfaction from playing again, even though my dexterity was no longer that of a teenage boy!

1983 was a sad year for my mother was ill with cancer and in a hospice in Leatherhead near my brother and his wife. I was keeping in touch and on a Friday asked Michael whether I should come but he judged that since she was in a coma it was probably not a good idea. However, I was convinced that I should go since I had not seen her for three months, so I booked a flight from Belfast to Gatwick for the Monday and I was met by my sister-in-law and driven to the hospice. With the Matron we all entered my mother's room and on the sound of voices she stirred. After a while the other two left me alone with my mother and after a short while she quietly died with me holding her hand. It was very special and peaceful. I was unable to attend her funeral due to my commitments in Northern Ireland (it was a long time before the Good Friday peace accords), but I felt that we had said goodbye in a much more personal and quiet way.

On the base we had a Chaplain, Niall Griffin and his wife Gerry, she from the North and he from the South having met at Dublin University. A delightful couple who became long term personal friends and who God used to reach out to us and convince us of our need of His divine friendship, and both Gillian and I became believers over the space of a few months, and we have never looked back or regretted anything. The experiences we had were very personal and we learnt a great deal whilst in NI and visited on many occasions the Renewal Centre at Rostrevor. It was a place where at that time, all creeds, genders, and spiritual disciplines would meet on equal not hierarchical terms for one purpose only – to worship God, which was far more than just singing songs! And so, Nuns would be beside Presbyterian ministers, lay people would be everywhere and nobody cared about who they were sitting next to or talking with. It was a grand time of unity in the faith. It all laid the foundations for much activity later on, particularly after we retired.

In 1984 an RAF Transport came through Aldergrove heading for the US. We managed to get seats on it to Dulles Airport where Bill Clark had left a car for us to use to drive up to Pennsylvania, and join him and his wife Julia on a trip to the air show at Oshkosh, WI, North of Chicago. This is probably the biggest airshow in the world involving current military and civil aircraft and helicopters of all types and eras, from WW1 to WW2 and since. The highlights were flying in a formation of 12 P51s to a resort SE of Oshkosh for a War Birds lunch outing, and of which I have the photos from the jockey seat of Bill's P51. Gillian also made the trip in a T6 Harvard flown by a dentist from New York!

When I think back it was a hell of a risk since what most P51 owners do is remove the fuel tank behind the pilot and put in a dicky seat, but you don't have a parachute, cannot reach any of the controls or even open the canopy. Not an experience for the ultra-cautious and nervous! Being able to get an FAA license on the basis of my CAA license plus a flight check in the worst aircraft I have ever flown called a Funk, meant that I was clear to fly Bill's aircraft at his personal airfield near State College PA. The FAA examiner, however, made up for it. A girl named MacKyntire, very attractive and an Air Hostess with United. Gillian and I had a great time and met some lovely people, including meeting up with an old RAF friend of mine, Darrol Stinton, who just happened to also be there.

The Funk by name and nature

Ecuador

In January 1985 I handed over command and we went home to Surrey to prepare for a move to Ecuador in South America, to the post of Defence Attache in the Embassy in Quito. This involved the usual sorting clothing, household equipment, and then briefings but above all language training in Spanish. At first it nearly drove me mad trying to grasp the basics but slowly we managed to get to grips with it and we had the help of a Colombian lady named Solly, married to an Englishman. She was also a Charismatic Catholic and we learnt a great deal through her about the Catholic Church and its beliefs and customs, which was a very good preparation for South America and its cultures and customs. Meeting other folk from Colombia was also very helpful, as was the fact that the Ambassador I was going to be working for also lived in Farnham and we were able to make social contact before we both went out to Ecuador. Michael and Veronica Atkinson became personal friends. We made the decision to get a Range Rover being a 4x4 vehicle and that proved to be a very smart decision, because it spent most of its life with us off road and up mountains and volcanoes. For this reason, we were able to see most of wild Ecuador well away from the touristy locations. I had had it equipped with dual fuel tanks and protective shields so that it would not sustain damage, since the roads were often more like tracks and very rough.

On arrival in Quito we were met by the Attache Corps all lined up with their wives which was very nice but a bit bewildering as we listened to all the different versions of Spanish being spoken. Not surprisingly we wondered if we had learned the right language! We moved into a hotel for two nights and then occupied the house allocated to us which was quite large and pleasant, and near the Embassy. There was some basic equipment in the house and Anita the maid was most helpful and over our time together we grew to love her like a daughter. The official car available to us was an American Ford Fairlane with a very soft swishy suspension but we used it to explore Quito a little. We also inherited a dog with the very original name 'Poochie' a very pretty Tibetan Terrier and a cat named Minnie. Then came the big event for two days after we arrived in Ecuador, on the evening of November 13th, around 9 p.m., the Nevada del Ruiz volcano in Colombia violently erupted. Within two to three hours, a fast-moving flow of mud, ice, rocks and lava called a lahar travelled more than 20 miles, burying towns and destroying the quite large town of Armero. The loss of life proved to be in excess of 23,000. I was immediately notified that I was to go to Colombia to command the British military contingent being sent to help with this disaster. So less than a week after setting foot in South America I was on my way via Bogota to the disaster area. It was really a tough call but one good thing came out of it in that our boxes, which contained my uniforms and equipment, appeared out of customs in a record short time, and with Gillian's help to find what I needed, I flew to Bogota on 17th and started to make all the necessary contacts. My British contingent consisted of an RAF Hercules transport which would be used to ferry aid from Bogota, where the international aid flights unloaded, to a Colombian Air Force base near to Armero. There were also two Puma helicopters which had flown down from Belize, the pilots of which I knew from my days at Odiham, a doctor, engineer, signallers and an Air Movements team which came with the Hercules. It was a joy to see these professionals take over the unloading and loading of all the aircraft at Bogota and give a lesson in how to do it to our Colombian hosts who had never before had to face that number of aircraft and the amount of freight.

In the event there was not a lot we could do in the way of rescue and the dividing line between life and death was very thin and abrupt. The material in the lahar is lethal being basically volcanic ash much like ground glass. To breathe it in or ingest it was a death sentence since it would cause internal bleeding on a scale for which there was no treatment. It was also impossible to float in it since it had the consistency of porridge. It was truly a tragic and overwhelming disaster. We had trouble with our communications but fortunately our American colleagues had effective satellite equipment and I was able to send messages through them to keep MOD and my Ambassador up to date as to the situation. One problem we had to cope with was to change a main rotor gearbox on one of the Pumas which was not easy given where we were and the lack of facilities, but we did get use of a hangar. So, it was flown in and the job done! I flew up the volcano in a US Blackhawk and we calculated that the lahar as it came down the mountain had been 300ft in depth and it filled a valley approximately 11 x 2 miles to a depth of 50 ft.

There were a few bodies and animals floating on the surface of the mud and who knows how many underneath it? We landed at Armero on the top of the ridge and there was a man standing there in T shirt boxer shorts and flip flops, I talked to him as best I could in my crude Spanish and learned that he had lost everything, house, wife, children and all he had left was what he was wearing. It was heartbreaking. The town of Armero is now a national monument and will never be rebuilt.

We did as much as we could, which turned out to be not anything near as much as we would have liked, and then I reported to the Colombian Air Force Chief of Staff before checking out with our Embassy in Bogota and getting a flight back to Quito. It was one of the hardest weeks of my life, both physically and emotionally. It was a great relief to walk into our house and normality, and to find that dear Gillian, aided by Anita, had already made it into a home, even to unpacking my clothes! In addition, our Range Rover had also arrived, so things started to look up with the help of Gonzalo my driver, of whom I became quite fond and was later able to help him and his family with a very difficult medical problem his little granddaughter experienced. My Ecuadorean secretary, Martha, although fluent in English, refused to allow me to speak other than Spanish with her and thus did me a great favour, because outside the Embassy and our English speaking friends, everything in my job was in Spanish. This was a great help when we were out in the remote parts of the country for I was able to talk to the locals and learnt a great deal about the people and their customs.

Cotopaxi

We walked and climbed extensively and found that lying in the pampas grass with a breeze blowing would again produce music just as it did in Kent forty years before. The notes were deeper, the grass longer but it was surprisingly peaceful up at 12,000 feet or above. We climbed Cotopaxi, one of the four perfect cone volcanoes in the world, and on these trips, we always had our trusty minder with us, Poochie the dog! Going up Cotopaxi she got to about 16,000feet and then stopped and would not go any farther having turned around and pointed herself downhill. It took us a while to work out what the problem was; the wind was flowing strongly downhill and kicking up the volcanic ash in a layer up to 18 inches above the ground. That is where she was right in the thick of it, and it was obviously not pleasant for her. So, Gillian stayed with her and protected her as best she could whilst I got up to the ice line at about 17,500feet. We did not have the right equipment to go any farther. That was the only time Poochie failed to keep up with us.

Gillian and Poochie on Pichincha Volcano

We arranged a trip to the Galapagos Islands in 1986, sailed from Guayaquil and went round all the islands on the ship which was very comfortable, and the wild life was a joy to watch. Pretty well all of these creatures were tame and very tolerant of humans, although they did demand that we walk round them and refused to get out of our way, which was reasonable since it was their home not ours. The land iguanas (average length 3 feet) would rear up against your leg and wait to be fed. Since their diet consisted mainly of cactus flowers, this was easily done. The three types of boobies (Gannets) were harmless and amusing, and one had to tread carefully round their nests on the ground. The red footed boobies were the only ones able to curl their flippers round branches and roost on shrubs and trees. The handsome masked boobies were the nearest in appearance to our European gannets. Californian sea lions abounded and were very entertaining with antics in the water, whilst the sea iguanas lay around on the rocks warming in the sun before diving again for their diet of lichen. The average time submerged for them was 20 minutes before cold and lack of air forced them out again. Galapagos penguins were dear little chaps and I was able to snorkel with them on one occasion. I kept trying to see what Darwin is supposed to have seen, evolution on a grand scale but all I could discern was animals, birds and insects, which had adapted to a new environment, but in other respects they were still the same as their land-based cousins. An amazing array of God's creation! I used 36 rolls of film during the time we were there, colour, colour slide and monochrome.

California Sea Lions

Blue Footed Booby nesting

And then in 1987 it was emergency time again with a 6.9 strength earthquake North East of Quito. This did a lot of physical damage with collapsed buildings and houses but the death toll was unknown for the major effect was on the Eastern slopes of the Andes and down into the Amazon basin. Sides of mountains took off and blocked a major river for 12 hours and the 18-inch oil pipeline from the basin over the mountains to Guayaquil, on the Pacific coast, looked as though a giant had just tied it into knots. I was put in charge of distributing the 50 tons of UK practical aid (tools, agricultural equipment, tents and protective plastic sheets) which came in on a civilian freight aircraft. To get it to where it was needed would take 5 large trucks and I had to negotiate with civil defence to get them, but even then the price was to turn a blind eye to one truck going to the CD barracks and not to the North. I realised then that I needed a reliable local partner to work with to get the aid to those who needed it most, so I went to the area of the disaster and met up with Mother Victoria who was a senior nun looking after the parish in the absence of a resident priest. It was a very wise choice and within a day or two tents and people working with tools on damaged buildings were to be seen everywhere. I had the utmost respect for my Catholic colleague. A major problem was that roofs would reach a harmonic and hurl their tiles off.

The choice of a Range Rover as a personal vehicle was very wise for it gave us freedom to go almost anywhere, but it was always equipped in the back with equipment designed to get us out of most kinds of difficulty or trouble, including sturdy planks for crossing broken bridges or fissures in the ground. We only had to dig ourselves out once as I recall, even though some of the roads would hardly have rated as footpaths! On one such trip way out in remote country to the North West of Quito on a mud road we came across a young couple walking along and stopped to give them a lift. It turned out that he was Ecuadorean American and she was American, probably in their mid to late twenties and very knowledgeable about the local area. We took them to their village and during lunch there, we met the local schoolmaster and heard all about the difficulties of keeping the young people in the area where they were needed because, to get training and a job, they had to go to the large towns. His ambition was to give them technical and workshop training which would give them skills useful to the local agricultural community. This caught my imagination and I resolved to see what we could do to help when we got back to Quito. I discussed it with my Ambassador and the Embassy staff, and we identified sources of funding available. I got the BAe manager interested too so we found that we could get enough funds together to provide a comprehensive workshop to kick start the programme. Some months later the machinery was delivered and we all drove to this remote area for the grand opening of the training programme. We were treated like Royalty and given the local delicacy at lunch – roast guinea pig. To be fair this was not your small cuddly children's pet type, but an animal technically a guinea pig but about the size of a large rabbit. Chickens came served with their legs and claws still attached!

Opening Day Celebration: British Ambassador Michael Atkinson second from right

Gillian and I got involved with various orphanages, one run by nuns in Quito which had a special heart for the babies abandoned on the streets or hidden in drains or dustbins. Some of these little people were real heartstring pullers, and we loved going to visit them. There was another larger orphanage to the North of Quito at Mitad del Mundo, so named since it was right on the Equator. These kids tended to be older, but had lost their parents and families in tragic circumstances. It was run by a Canadian pastor, John Munday, with whom I became quite close and in fact it was where I was baptised. Being who and what I was created quite a stir and a number of the kids joined in and were also baptised. I remember one little boy of about ten, sitting beside me as we waited and he was an orphan. His father, a policeman had been shot dead by bandits and his mother very soon after that had died of cancer. That was a typical story and since there was no such thing as social services or the National Health Service, life was very tough and sometimes cruel for many. I kept in touch and supported John for some ten years after leaving Ecuador until he died in the late 90s.

I did manage to visit one of the many slightly illegal gold mines in the South West of the country. This involved a climb through thick mud up to a height of about 3,000 feet amsl. It was just like the Wild West. Very basic machines and methods of extracting the gold, and a community with the benefit? of a saloon, with girls and women who did laundry, served bar and food, and were available on a personal basis. The men who smelted the ore using mercury to separate the gold, would burn off the mercury over a Bunsen flame, and the mercury fumes were being breathed in. It was obvious from my observations that these men were physically there, but not mentally for the eyes were dead. I suppose they would qualify as being 'mad as a hatter'. Getting the ingots out and down the mountain was fraught with danger, and there had been many robberies at gunpoint, and some deaths, so the couriers were always escorted by armed guards or private armies. It was a little easier going back downhill but not much and I have to admit that at the end of the day I was exhausted.

One good thing that came out of this tour was the making of long-term friends amongst the military attachés. Colonel Shabtay ben-Shoa of the Israeli Air Force was a particularly good friend and we discussed many deep things together, both secular and spiritual. He had flown in two wars 1967 and the 1973 Yom Kippur. It was an honour and of great interest to attend his son's Bar Mitzvah. Sadly, Shabtay was killed in an air crash in Quito three weeks after we left Ecuador and came home to the UK in 1988. Colonel Rick Flores, US Army, was a Puerto Rican, small and stocky but with a chest full of medals for bravery, he had spent a lot of time in Special Forces and we visited on both sides of the Atlantic. Colonel Gary Lape US Air Force was an A10 operator and wing commander with wide experience and we visited him and his wife in Tucson and hosted them for a tourist tour of London. Captain Mike McGrath USN was a special guy who flew Phantoms over North Vietnam, was shot down, and spent six years in what was euphemistically known as the 'Hanoi Hilton', a prisoner of war camp like no other for its cruelty and murder. He recorded his experiences in a book of drawings 'Prisoner of War – Six Years in Hanoi' published by the Naval Institute Press. ISBN 0-87021-527-2. Gillian and Marlene McGrath had a special bond in that they both were tossed together into the Pacific off Esmeraldas when the gangway of the Ecuadorean Navy Sail

Training Ship collapsed and it was at least a twelve-foot drop. Fortunately, they both were good swimmers, but Gill lost her spectacles and couldn't see anything without them. Her bruising was testament to the fact that she had bounced off the tender waiting to take us ashore! We visited with all of these guys and their wives both in the US and here in the UK. I still have contact with those who have survived.

My responsibilities and activies in Ecuador were mainly sales related but I did have a watching brief on the activities of the Colombian drug cartels who had coca factories in the Ecuadorean jungle, but because of their location and protection it was very difficult to deal with them, and would take resources that the Ecuadoreans did not have. We experienced a number of other events we remembered with pleasure and interest: trips down the Napo River, a tributary of the Amazon, to a camp in the jungle. Very basic, bamboo huts on stilts, insects, snakes and troublesome monkeys. The canoe trips downriver were exhilarating and dangerous, particularly in or near the rainy season when the flow is high and turbulent. The 'canoes' are hollowed out tree trunks, varying in length (thirty to sixty feet) and width (four to six feet), with powerful outboards on the stern. If one were to become breached across the flow, despite the thickness of their hulls, they would be snapped in two, and empty their passenger/freight into the river. This happened to one canoe just ahead of us and we picked up some of the survivors.

Treks in the rain forest were hard going and we learnt not to bother with rain gear but wear what the natives did, trousers or shorts and a shirt or T shirt and when the rain stops just dry out naturally. However, boots were a good idea and keeping an eye open ahead of you on the ground and above you in the trees was essential. Animals and snakes will usually only attack in self defence except for the larger boas and especially the anaconda which is not only a good swimmer but a good tree climber too, which is amazing considering its size and weight. It has a habit of lying on a branch above a track and dropping on its prey, which normally is all that is needed. Coral snakes, although with lethal venom, have the most beautiful coloured skin. On one occasion Gillian was having a shower (river water, brown and gavity fed) and screamed because a large (over two inches) cockroach had joined her for a bath. Whilst dealing with this emergency I noticed a shieldbug very similar to the little green chaps we have here, but three inches across. I didn't tell Gillian about that one! Although they were there in the rivers, we did not see crocodiles or piranhas. We had already seen huge sixteen foot crocs in India. In all our stays abroad we naturally had many family and friends visiting and Ecuador was no exception, but was more challenging because of the need to get accustomed to the altitude.

Home and MOD Three

We left Quito by an American Airlines flight to Miami where we would pick up a BA Flight to London. It was May 1988 and our hearts were heavy having left Anita whom we loved, and the animals who had been our companions for nearly three years. The dog Poochie, had taken it very hard and we hated leaving her but for many reasons it was impractical to bring her back to the UK. We were met at Heathrow by a sales rep from the Volvo garage in Farnham from which we had ordered a new car, a 345 to supplement my old 144S stored in the garage of our house. Having been away so long there was a tremendous amount to do getting re-established in our own home. The whole establishment, which wasn't very big anyway had been looked after and managed by a friend and neighbour and we had paid her for her efficient services. It took some time to acclimatise to the temperatures and the lower altitude which surprised us, but it was a great relief to be home at last and I knew that I did not have to report to my new job until July. This was a post at the Defence Operational Analysis Establishment in West Byfleet and I would, once in post, be able to easily commute either by train or car. It was only going to be for nine months since I would be retiring in 1989 at the ripe old age of 55. It was an interesting time learning the analysis techniques, and becoming familiar with computers, since the whole enterprise was based on a huge VAX mainframe computer living in a very large air-conditioned room, or rather hall! I set about learning as much as I could about computers, and software, and how to use them and was greatly helped by my civilian colleagues whom I suppose you would call Boffins. I quickly bought my own first basic machine but within a short time had graduated to faster and a more capable 386, then a 486, and Pentium, then moving into the building and upgrading of them, which helped many folks later, since I was also able to teach people how to use them. However, the job did involve trips into MOD in London to go to meetings and conferences so it was quite a busy time. Gillian was very happy to be back in her own home and we caught up with friends and my brother who had returned to the UK at last to work in Shell Centre, and conveniently lived in Dorking, fairly near to Farnham. He had had an interesting time in Africa and the Middle East and had been the Shell operations Manager in Libya at the time of the Col Gaddafi coup. Negotiating with the new regime was challenging. Sadly, he died young in 2007 aged 74 from lupus which had quite quickly demolished his immune system and then attacked some of his vital organs. Not a pretty end.

I continued in the Service until the end of March 1989 and then retired on June 15th handing in all my personal equipment, then we both took a deep breath and said, "What now?" On the 9th November the Berlin Wall came down and heralded the end of the Soviet Union and thus also the end of the Cold War which I had been fighting in various ways for all my career. In a way this was also answered for us in that a friend, Peter White, out of the blue asked if he could bunk with us whilst working with a church in Aldershot, and he and I started working together on producing Christian audio and video tapes. A few months later he brought Brenda to meet us and they were married in 1991. Sadly, Peter died in 1997 but Brenda, who is a distinguished pianist under the name of Brenda McDermott, has been a very close friend for both Gillian and me ever since. It also introduced us to some of the local churches and later as my computer skills increased I found myself running French adapted computers to a church complex in France in the Vendee region close to La Rochelle. We also became involved with counselling and helping people with problems, and had taken a number of courses to equip us to do so. This also applied in the area of marriage, and we felt that we had had so much blessing in our lives and our time together as a couple, that we wanted to give something back. This was a very busy time for us and we were rarely at home at weekends being anywhere in England and even up in Scotland. We met some lovely people who we were able to help and doing all this helped us too!

We made numerous trips to the USA to see our friends there and travelled fairly widely from the East to the West coast and enjoyed Virginia, Maryland, Texas, Arizona, Wisconsin and California. It was great to be back on familiar ground, but sadly our friend Bill Clark from State College Pennsylvania had been killed in an air crash in March 1988 and his immaculate P51 was lost too. A sad time, for he was a nice and generous guy, and a difficult time for Julia his wife whom we did see. I bought a mountain bike around this time and went 'off road' on the wilder areas of Surrey in the Farham, Aldershot and Guildford areas. It was challenging but great fun if also a little dangerous in the steep wooded places. In 1994 the Orrs, our long standing and close friends, were resident in Edinburgh, she being the US Consul General in Scotland, and we, with the Bryants, another American couple, went to see them. We drove up through the heart of England, where the Peak and Lake Districts were of particular interest to the Bryants. On arrival in Edinburgh we found that they had other guests staying, John and Sue Young. John a distinguished astronaut, then having the most time in space, approximately 37 days and had been on Gemini, Apollo, the Shuttle and on the moon. He was on a speaking tour in Scotland and sitting at breakfast one morning he asked what I had done. So, amongst other details I mentioned Australia, Maralinga and Christmas Island. He asked me what I had done there and I explained about flying through the nuclear clouds and the sampling. He looked me straight in the eye and said, "Gee that's brave," and he wasn't joking. That coming from him, or indeed from any of his astronaut colleagues, was really an accolade for all the guys like myself, pilots and navigators, who had flown those sampling missions. I have it on good authority that at the time of writing this there are only nine of us left, age and ill health having taken our colleagues.

I still played the oboe I had bought in Northern Ireland and teamed up with an old friend Peter Penfold who had been at Cranwell with me but was now retired and living near Carmarthen. He had taken up the saxophone. Tenor, alto and baritone playing in a local band, and so, as well as playing pétanque over gin and tonics, we got together, transposed music to suit the instruments, and played together. We were told by our wives that the sound wafting through the trees (we were playing in their wood) was magical. Both

Peter and his wife were very good potters and had their own mini pottery with kiln, and produced some attractive items which I still have. Sadly, he died in 2003 so that virtually ended my musical career.

In 1996 we had moved from Surrey to East Devon where we both worked with a number of Christian charities near Axminster and later in Seaton. The house we had bought was right on the East Devon West Dorset border, and so walking was just outside the door and a ten-mile hike was quite usual, as was an eight-mile round trip down to Lyme Regis to get an ice cream and return. It was when out walking and climbing a very steep hill with long grass, that something felt very wrong with me and my heart, and I had difficulty making it back home. Very slow investigations by the NHS eventually showed the need for a triple bypass op on my heart and, to celebrate my 70th birthday, we went up to London where, in the London Heart hospital, I was successfully dealt with. At one point it was touch and go in the ICU as I developed a reaction to morphine, but fortunately I got over it and we were home in Devon after eight days. Recovery was gradual, but I was determined to get back to normal with walking and cycling as soon as I could. A change in diet away from animal products was a wise move to prevent a recurrence. In that hospital I identified eighteen different nationalities, including some cleaners who were Ecuadorean so I was able to practise my Spanish.

In anticipation of the heart op we had moved to a flat in Farringdon very near Exeter airport. This was convenient for flights to Spain and access to the M5 and the A30/A38 deeper into Devon and Cornwall. Here we made many friends and our good friends Michael and Shirley Hynds had already moved into a flat there a year before. We took many trips with them, mainly to and in Spain where they had an Apartment and it was great fun to explore Andalucia and practicing my now rusty Spanish. So, life towards the end of our time was quiet and a welcome change from the sometimes-hectic activities of the previous nearly fifty years. We managed a few SAGA cruises which were enjoyable despite some violent storms, but it seemed an expensive way to see a little of the world, for after all we had seen a great deal already in our travels. After our constant moves around the world it was nice to be more stationary. So life was pleasant but low key which suited us both until February 28th 2018 when Gillian had a major stroke. Fortunately, I managed to get her into hospital within the hour, even though it was 2am, but it was two months before she could be released to come home, and during that time I had prepared our flat to cope with her disabilities and been to see her in the Stroke Ward pretty well every day. By observation and planning I was prepared for her return on May 2nd, but from then on it was a steep learning curve for both of us. We had excellent help from an NHS Stroke Support Team and I knew how to use the specialist machines. On the advice of a physiotherapist we acquired <u>Fred the Therapy Bear</u> to protect Gillian's chest from a now rigid left arm and hand. I made two promises to Gillian: if at all possible she would not go into a home and I would look after her for as long as I could. I kept them!

Fred Therapy in Covid Lockdown

So life's pattern changed and became much slower yet more intense, but we managed to build some normality into it and moving Gillian around in the car was at that time relatively easy. As time went on and she slowly became less mobile we had to curtail our activities, but still managed visits to local friends and pubs. In time an electric wheelchair and then a WAV (wheelchair accessible vehicle) became necessary for I was now in my late 80s and my strength was declining. I still managed to care for and move Gillian around daily but eventually after her fourth stay in hospital, her needs became beyond my capabilities. She needed two people to safely move her from bed to chair and back. The last time she was still really my Gillian was June 14th 2023 when we were taken out to lunch by friends to celebrate my birthday, but she faded quite rapidly and unexpectedly died in the A&E dept of RD&E Hospital on 29th July. I think it would be quite realistic to say that my life came to a grinding halt at that moment and I have constantly missed her ever since, but I have not stopped making every effort to get back to some sort of normality. Even writing this account of my life!!

Gillian

Gillian. By now it must be more than clear that in most of this journey I was not alone, and I had a companion, helper, mentor, partner of whom it is difficult for me to make objective judgements because our lives were so willingly intertwined. To say that we were, and still are, welded at head, heart and hip, is simplistic perhaps but a statement of fact. I don't suppose that either of us realised at the start that we would become so meshed, but all I can say is that she was the best thing that could ever have happened to me. Did we have our downs as well as ups? Certainly, we did and had the same difficulties overcoming them as other folk, but we were committed to doing so and as time went on we became stronger and the downs became fewer. We could do little about the medical problems that beset both of us at times, but we were always there to help each other recover, especially from the life threatening ones. She had had to have a full hysterectomy in Germany in 1963 and we had both agreed to it knowing that we would never have children. As I told her, "I didn't marry you just to have children, nice as that would have been, I married you because you are YOU," for her gynaecological problems had made life very difficult and painful for her.

Us in 1994

She was surprisingly talented in a quiet way. She made her own dresses, painted (was quite a good forger of Picasso), was an excellent cook, had modelled semi-professionally, was interested in and knowledgeable about wildlife and was very interested in botany. Her grandfather, with whom she spent a great deal of time when she was a little girl, was a botanist and chemist of note having received three silver medals from the Royal Society for his work in these fields. From him she learnt the Latin names of most plants and flowers and later did a course at RHS Wisley when we lived in Surrey. Add an interest in, and knowledge of, rocks, fossils and sea shells, and the spectrum of her interests was very wide. We shared a wide taste in music ranging from classical through to modern jazz. She was also an excellent hostess.

Gillian Modelling

    She was always so welcoming of others and smiled so readily, not to mention her roguish sense of humour which, together with mine, would have us in fits of laughter in no time. We were always so glad to see each other again after enforced absences, and I never felt complete when she was not with me. She was also strong willed and was no pushover when she felt strongly about something, and she disliked and would resist folk who tried to dominate her just because she tended to be quiet and sometimes rather shy. With hindsight, I realise that she was, in fact, a precious gift to me and our union was arranged for us, so who can say that arranged marriages don't work that well, for this one did! I had my heart broken twice, once when she had her major stroke in 2018 and I had to watch her slowly fade away over the nearly six years that I nursed her, and then again when she died in 2023 at the age of 93. But the memories of her are grand!

Conclusion

So what is the conclusion? Is it Hagar the Horrible caught in a storm at sea, OR the wisdom of Solomon in Ecclesiastes? For me it is the latter with grateful thanks for a full and long life with many enriching and shared experiences:

Ecc 12:13 -14 Let us hear the conclusion of the whole matter: Fear God and keep His commandments, For this is man's all. For God will bring every work into judgment, Including every secret thing, Whether good or evil.

www.ingramcontent.com/pod-product-compliance
Lightning Source LLC
Chambersburg PA
CBHW041219070526
44584CB00001B/21